Road, Bed, Two,
The Rise and Fall of Little Voice

Road: 'A surreal vision of the contemporary urban landscape . . . uncomfortable and magical, funny and bitter. It is a northern *Under Milk Wood*, high on pills and booze.' *Sunday Times*

'An original, affecting, rumbustious and truly remarkable piece of work, let alone a superb first play.' Michael Coveney, *Financial Times*

Bed: 'Cartwright writes better about old people than anyone I know, except perhaps Beckett. This is an odd, harrowing and hilarious piece, entirely without sentimentality, sturdy but moving.' John Peter, *Sunday Times*

Two: 'A sharp, salty quickfire evocation of the surface gaiety and underlying melancholia of English pub life.' Michael Billington, *Guardian*

'This extraordinary gifted and original voice . . . populates the space with broad humour, dry wit and often shudderingly moving poetry.' Steve Grant, *Time Out*

The Rise and Fall of Little Voice: 'A cracker, original, hilarious and hauntingly sad . . . Jim Cartwright is one of the mavericks of British theatre.' Charles Spencer, *Daily Telegraph*

Jim Cartwright lives in Lancashire, where he was born. *Road*, his first play, won the Samuel Beckett Award 1986, *Drama* magazine award 1986, was joint winner of the George Devine Award 1986 and *Plays and Players* Award 1986. The TV version won the Golden Nymph Award for the best film at the Monte Carlo Television Festival. His other plays include: *Bed* (National Theatre, Cottesloe, 1989) and *Two* (Bolton Octagon, 1989 and Young Vic, London, 1990), winner of the *Manchester Evening News* Best New Play Award in 1990. *The Rise and Fall of Little Voice* won the *Evening Standard* Best Comedy Award in 1992 and the 1993 Olivier Award for Best Comedy. In 1996 he directed his play *I Licked a Slag's Deodorant* for the Royal Court at the Ambassadors Theatre, London.

Methuen Contemporary Dramatists
include

Peter Barnes (three volumes)
Sebastian Barry
Edward Bond (six volumes)
Howard Brenton
  (two volumes)
Richard Cameron
Jim Cartwright
Caryl Churchill (two volumes)
Sarah Daniels (two volumes)
David Edgar (three volumes)
Dario Fo (two volumes)
Michael Frayn (two volumes)
Peter Handke
Jonathan Harvey
Declan Hughes
Terry Johnson
Bernard-Marie Koltès
Doug Lucie
David Mamet (three volumes)

Anthony Minghella
  (two volumes)
Tom Murphy (four volumes)
Phyllis Nagy
Peter Nichols (two volumes)
Philip Osment
Louise Page
Stephen Poliakoff
  (three volumes)
Christina Reid
Philip Ridley
Willy Russell
Ntozake Shange
Sam Shepard (two volumes)
David Storey (three volumes)
Sue Townsend
Michel Vinaver (two volumes)
Michael Wilcox

JIM CARTWRIGHT

Plays: 1

Road
Bed
Two
The Rise and Fall of Little Voice

Methuen Drama

METHUEN CONTEMPORARY DRAMATISTS

This edition first published in Great Britain 1996
by Methuen Drama
215 Vauxhall Bridge Road, London SW1V 1EJ

10 9 8 7

Road first published in Great Britain in 1986 by Methuen Drama in the
Royal Court Writers series and reissued in this revised version in the
Methuen Modern Plays series in 1990. Copyright © 1986, 1990 by Jim
Cartwright
Bed first published in Great Britain in 1991 by Methuen Drama reissued
with corrections in a volume with *Two* in 1994. Copyright © 1991, 1994
by Jim Cartwright
Two first published in Great Britain as *To* in 1991 by Methuen Drama;
reissued with corrections in a volume with *Bed* in 1994. Copyright ©
1991, 1994, by Jim Cartwright
The Rise and Fall of Little Voice first published in Great Britain in 1992;
reissued with corrections in 1994. Copyright © 1992 by Jim Cartwright

Copyright in this collection © 1996 by Jim Cartwright
Jim Cartwright has asserted his right under the Copyright, Designs and
Patents Act, 1988 to be identified as the author of this work.

ISBN 0-413-70230-8

A CIP catalogue record for this book is available from the British Library

Typeset by Wilmaset Ltd, Birkenhead, Wirral
Printed and bound in Great Britain by
Cox & Wyman Ltd, Reading, Berkshire

Contents

Chronology

1986   *Road* produced at the Royal Court Theatre,
London; subsequently toured Britain. It won the
Samuel Beckett Award and *Drama* magazine's Best
New Play Award, was joint winner of the George
Devine Award and *Plays and Players* Award.

1987   BBC TV version of *Road*. It won the Golden
Nymph Award for Best Film at the Monte Carlo
Television and Film Festival.
Baths, a radio play, broadcast on BBC Radio 4.

1988   *Vroom*, a film, 'Centrepiece' at the London Film
Festival and shown on Channel 4.

1989   *Bed* produced at the Royal National Theatre,
London
Two, first produced as *To*, at the Octagon Theatre,
Bolton. It won the Manchester *Evening News* Best
New Play Award and transferred the following year
to the Young Vic, London.

1990   *June and Wedded*, two plays for television,
transmitted on BBC TV.

1992   *The Rise and Fall of Little Voice* opened at the
Cottesloe, Royal National Theatre, London,
subsequently transferring to the Aldwych Theatre.
It won the 1992 *Evening Standard* Best Comedy
Award and 1993 Olivier Award for Best Comedy.

1996   *I Licked a Slag's Deodorant* directed by the author
for the Royal Court at the Ambassadors Theatre,
London.

Road

Road was first performed at the Royal Court Theatre Upstairs, London, on 22 March 1986, with the following cast:

Scullery	Edward Tudor-Pole
Carol's Mother	Susan Brown
Carol	Mossie Smith
Louise	Leslie Sharp
Brink	Neil Dudgeon
Eddie's Dad	Colin McCormack
Eddie	William Armstrong
Molly	Susan Brown
Professor	Colin McCormack
Skin	William Armstrong
Helen	Susan Brown
Jerry	Colin McCormack
Joey	Neil Dudgeon
Clare	Lesley Sharp

All other parts played by members of the company.

Directed by Simon Curtis
Produced by Max Stafford-Clark
Designed by Paul Brown

Road transferred to the Royal Court's main auditorium on 9 June 1986 with the above cast and returned in January 1987 with the following changes:

Scullery	Ian Dury
Louise	Jane Horrocks
Brother	Ewan Stewart
Brenda	Susan Brown
Carol	Mossie Smith
Brink	Ewan Stewart
Eddie	Iain Glen
Eddie's Dad	Alan David
Molly	Susan Brown
Professor	Alan David
Chantal	Mossie Smith
Skin	Iain Glen
Jerry	Alan David
Clare	Jane Horrocks
Joey	Ewan Stewart
Helen	Susan Brown
Valerie	Jane Horrocks

All other parts played by members of the company.

The Place: a road in a small Lancashire town.

The time: tonight.

Note on Pre-Show and Interval

There was a pre-show (described on p. 5) to the Royal Court production. If this is not used the play begins with Act One.

A development of the Royal Court's main auditorium production was a disco in the theatre and entertainment in the bar during the interval. If this is not used, the Interval section in the play (p. 47 to p. 49) can be cut but then the second scene in Act Two (the chip shop scene, p. 50 to p. 51) should also be cut so that the first scene with Scullery and the musical box moves immediately to the third scene where Dor and Lane appear high up eating chips.

Pre-Show

In the street in front of the theatre, **Chantal** *(a young girl from Road, about sixteen but simple-minded) is hanging around or going up and down on a little child's shove scooter. After a while she is joined by* **Linda** *(another girl from Road, about twelve). She is in her night-dress and has sneaked out to play before going to bed. They sit on the theatre steps and play chalk games, sometimes obscene. As the time for the performance approaches, the House Manager of the theatre should come out and tell them to clear off.*

As this is occurring outside, inside the theatre bar has been converted into the Millstone Pub, *a typical old Lancashire pub, with a dartboard, a little tiny stage in the corner, with mike and glitter ribbons behind for the pub entertainers to perform on, posters advertising the 'Pub Disco Room' with 'Bisto and His Beatoven Disco', pub lunches, trips, photographs advertising tonight's turns: 'Chance Peterson, singer', 'Tom Stanley, your compère', 'The Electric Clutch, erotic dancers', etc. The following scene was used as a basis for the bar improvisation; it should be noted this is a scene only to be passed through or by, and not the start of the play and should be very low-key, slow, natural and lengthy, almost unnoticeable.*

Barry *is in the pub playing darts.*

Brenda *comes in and goes to the bar.*

Brenda Hey mate. Can I have a drink ont' slate, eh. Summat ont' slate. I'm skint you see, until me daughter gi's me some later. She comes in here, Carol, you know her. Gi'us one an she'll pay you later. Eh. Eh. Go on lovey, gi'us a bottle. Oh sod off then. Stuck up flea. *(She turns round and sees* **Barry**.) Barry! Baz! Playin' darts then Baza.

He ignores her.

What time is it, Bar?

Barry Dunno.

Brenda What ha'you doing in so early, Bar?

He ignores her.

Eh? What's so early for?

Barry I'm waiting for John to play pool.

Brenda Aye, lend us a cig.

He plays on.

A cig, Bar.

He plays on.

Lend us a cig.

Barry *gives her one. He plays on.*

Brenda Got a light, Bar.

He plays.

Got a light, Barry?

He throws his lighter at her, plays on. She picks it up, lights up, pockets the lighter. She watches the game.

Brenda Want a pound on one?

He ignores her. She watches.

Wan' a pound on one?

He ignores, she watches.

Wan' a pound on one?

Barry BLOODY HELL!

Brenda Do you though, Bar?

Barry EH!

Brenda Want a pound on one. I've no drink money, does see Bar? But it might be me lucky day eh? Might it Bar?

Barry Alreet then. (*He starts walking to the bar.*)

Brenda Reet. God I've gone thirsty I always do when I'm coming up to play.

Barry (*to the* **Barman**) 'Nother set o' darts, cock.

The **Barman** *passes them over the bar to* **Barry. Brenda** *is disappointed — she thought he was going for drinks.*

Here. (*He shoves them in her hand.*)

They go to the board and play the first set.

Brenda You chalk up Bar, I can't do take-aways.

As he goes up to the blackboard, she takes a quick sip of his drink. They play another set. She's waiting for him to go to the board again. But this time he downs his drink in one then goes to the board to chalk up.

Brenda Do you want another then, Barry? (*To the* **Barman.**) He might want another here in a sec, love.

Barry *is returning.*

Brenda Do you, Bar?

Barry What?

Brenda Want another ale.

Barry Shut up an' play if you're playing.

Brenda I'll have to whether I want to or not, won't a? I need that pound more than me next breath Baz, I'll tell you that. I mean remember you're playing a girl.

He's gone. He is over at the bar queuing for a drink. She sneakily runs up and shoves the darts in the board, then runs back to her spot.

Brenda One hundred and eighty! One hundred and eighty! Look at that, Barry, look.

Barry *goes to the board, takes the darts out.*

Barry Game's over.

Brenda Eh?

Barry Game's over Brenda.

Brenda Well what about 50p for a good try?

Barry (*carrying on playing on his own*) Go.

Brenda *runs in front of the dartboard.*

Barry Move Brenda or I'll throw this right in the cow's eye.

Brenda (*beaten, under her breath*) Fuck you.

She goes.

Meanwhile, in the auditorium **Scullery** *is there on stage or on the floor to greet the audience as they come in. On stage* **Eddie's Dad** *is in his house, sitting on an armchair, fixing a Hoover across his knee, the TV on. In another house,* **Louise's Brother** *is sitting on a chair fixing an oily engine.* **Brenda** *enters her house and sits in an armchair smoking, tense. When all the audience are in and settled, Act One begins.*

Act One

Somewhere Over the Rainbow by Judy Garland is playing. The record ends.

Blackness.

A match is struck. It is held underneath a broken road sign. The name part has been ripped off, leaving a sharp, twisted, jagged edge, only the word 'Road' is left. The sign is very old and has been this way a long time.

Scullery It's been broken.

The flame moves across to illuminate a man's face. He holds the match there until it goes out; at the same time a spotlight creeps up on his face.

Wid' your night yous chose to come and see us. Wid' our night as usual we's all gettin' ready and turning out for a drink. THIS IS OUR ROAD! But tonight it's your road an' all! Don't feel awkward wi' us, make yourselves at home. You'll meet 'all-sorts' down here, I'm telling you love. An' owt can happen tonight. He might get a bird. She might ha' a fight, she might. Let's shove off downt' Road and find out! We'll go down house by house. Hold tight! Here we go! Come on! (*He beckons the audience around*). Watch the kerb missus! Road's coming round us! (*He starts laughing, laughing uproariously.*)

*Blackout, then the lights come up on a living-room. There is a mirror up at the back. A man, **Louise's Brother**, in a vest and old black trousers and socks, is sitting in a chair, leaning over and working on an oily engine, on spread-out newspapers.*

*A young girl, **Louise**, bursts in, dressed for going out, frantically brushing her hair.*

Louise Late, late again, late. Can I get to mirror?

Brother Shut it.

She has to try and do it from where she is.

Louise Where's Mum and Dad?

Brother (*mouths*) Shagging.

Louise Is they?

He looks at her in disbelief, shakes his head, carries on.

I wish to God you wun't joke me like that. I could just imagine 'em there then, on that dirty bed of vests.

He just ignores her, carries on.

You not going out?

He stares at her. She jumps in fear. She carries on brushing. She looks round.

Where's dog?

Brother Out back.

Louise Have you fed him today?

Brother (*not looking up*) Fuck facey, fuck facey. Fuck facey. Fuck facey. Fuck off. Fuck off.

Louise Why do you never go out, you?

Brother Can't afford it. Why do you never stay in?

Louise I can't stand it.

Brother *throws the engine at her. She jumps back, screams.*

Louise You think you're scary. But you're just a big lump of it.

Brother *turns the chair over.*

Brother (*sexual*) Let's dance.

Louise (*scared*) You can't dance with your brother.

Brother I know. Everything's not allowed in life. (*He takes two quid out, gives it to her.*) Here.

Louise Where's that from?

Brother (*indicating the engine*) I'm doing a job for Eric.

Louise (*holding the money*) You go an' get a pint on it.

Brother No, I've got a quarter-bottle under me pillow.

Louise You're not going back to bed is you, you're there all day and night.

Brother Do you want a punch?

Louise No.

Brother I wish you did. I'd love to see summat' go down. (*He looks at his oily hands.*) I'm going for a bath.

Louise Don't put the immersion on, me mum 'ull kill you.

He puts his hands on her face. Then draws them down her cheeks, smudging make-up and leaving black.

Oh no! I'm goin' be really late now. I'm going have go up and do it again. I'm goin' be late late now. You pigging bastard.

She goes up.

He looks out after her, starts clapping, clapping his hands for a long time. He suddenly stops.

Brother (*blankly to the audience*) Fucking long life in' it?

Blackout.

The lights come up on another living-room. An old beaten red armchair, an ironing-board up at the back. **Brenda**, *a thin wizened scruffy woman, sits in the chair facing the audience, smoking. At the back,* **Carol**, *in bra and knickers, is ironing her dress.*

Brenda (*speaks in a low, quiet, one-tone voice*) Where you goin'?

Carol Out.

Brenda Where you goin'?

Carol Out.

Brenda Where you goin'?

Carol The pub.

Brenda Tha's better. What time you be back?

Carol Whenever.

Brenda What time you be back?

Carol Whenever.

Brenda What time?

Carol Eleven, twelve-ish.

Brenda Tha's better. Are you still seeing that lad?

Carol I'm not answering any more questions.

Brenda There you are then. Don't bring anyone back here the night.

Carol As though I would.

Brenda You would. You would. I'm sick of the sound of it down here.

Carol What do you mean?

Brenda You know.

Carol Look leave me alone, I'm ironing this.

Brenda Well speak then.

Carol Look why should I eh? You're nothing to me.

Brenda I'm mother.

Carol You're my mother so what?

Brenda I'm your mother and I brung you from . . . (*She indicates with her hand.*) . . . that to that!

Carol Aye, aye, well I'm leaving soon. So thanks an' all that, but there you are.

Brenda Aye here I am, and there you are, so let's have something.

Carol What?

Brenda Respect and money.

Carol I'll give you your money Monday morning and your respect's down the bog.

Brenda Pissing young git.

There is the sound of someone shouting and laughing. They both get up and lean out front.

Carol
Brenda } *(together)* SHUT IT!!

They look at each other and laugh. They go back to ironing and sitting.

Brenda Have you had 'owt eat?

Carol I've had a warmed-up pastie from dinner.

Brenda Well get summat else.

Carol What else? There's rock all in, but shrunk carrots, Sugar Puffs, and some spit or summat in a saucer.

Brenda Don't exaggerate.

Carol Uh.

Brenda Anyway get summat down you before you go out.

Carol You get summat down you.

Brenda You get summat down you.

Carol You get summat down you.

Brenda You get summat down you.

Carol You get summat down you.

Brenda You get summat down you.

Carol You get summat down you. You're the one who's goin' to be pissed up and lying in it.

Brenda Shove it you little tart.

Carol You shove it.

Carol *turns the dress over, spits on the iron, carries on.*

Brenda So you're goin' down the boozer are you?

Carol Yeah. Are you?

Brenda I might go down if somebody coughs up.

Carol Are you still going with that ragman?

Brenda No.

Carol Why not?

Brenda He snotted off din't he. He owes me an' all.

Carol Eh?

Brenda Yeah like you all do, every one of yous. I s'pose you're skint an' all?

Carol Well I've got some but I need it for tonight.

Brenda Well give it me.

Carol No.

Brenda Yes.

Carol No.

Brenda Yes.

Carol No.

Brenda Yes.

Carol No, you mouldy old slag.

Brenda Yes, you young pig.

Carol Cow!

Brenda Sick!

Carol Oh God, you're crude. How could I have let you bring me up. Fling me up more like, I was flung through the years.

Brenda Listen her romanticising. You've done all right out of my bones you lot.

Carol You're nothing but bones anyway. Why don't you eat?

Brenda Because I don't. Because I don't. I do anyway. I get enough.

Carol You'd rather swill ale. Wun't you? Look at you. Your skin's like ham. There's veins showing all over you. You're hung in your old clothes. You never wash, you never change. You never . . . never . . . (*She can't bring herself to say it.*) I'm like I am because of you and you're like you are because of who knows what rot. (*She puts her dress on. It is very short.*) Is it short enough for you?

Brenda Ask men.

A loud knocking on the door.

Carol Come in Louise!

Carol *puts her coat on.*

Louise *comes in, she looks upset.*

Louise (*to both*) Hello.

Brenda (*uninterested*) Hiyah.

Carol (*to Louise*) What's up with you?

Louise Me shoulder pad's slipped.

Carol Pissing hell Louise, there's always summat wi' you.

They set off.

Brenda Are you giving me some?

Carol I can let you have a pound.

Brenda Oh generous. Generous. Generosity. Generosity. Generous.

Carol *throws change all over the floor, then walks out with Louise.*

Brenda *scurries and scrambles on the floor for money. She stops on all fours, looks to the audience.*

Brenda Fucking long life in' it.

The lights come up on the Road.

Scullery *enters, with a bottle.*

Scullery All right? (*He nods to someone in the audience, offers a drink to another.*) Do you want one, luv? (*He drinks.*) This is my domain. I'm in and out everywhere here, all about. There's everything you needs, two pubs at the top, chippy round the side, places to hide. This road and me. (*He pours some rum on the Road.*) Have one. What a fuckin' place though!

Carol *and* **Louise** *pass.*

Carol *The Millstone. The Swan. The Blue Boar. The New Zealand Chief. Ikkey's. Wheatsheaf. Gypsy's Tent.*

Louise *White Horse. Market. Ancient Shepherd. Smokey's. The Millstone.*

Scullery My darlings.

They run off squealing and laughing.

Carol (*off*) Fuck off, Scullery!

Scullery Come an' taste me!

Carol (*shouting off*) No way, your fly's full of fleas!

Scullery Please yourself, chickens. You can't escape! (*He blows a kiss after them, winks then drinks.*) Let me help you get your bearings. There's the town, there's this Road, then there's the slag heap. This is the last stop. All of life is chucked here. You've seen nowt yet. There's auld Molly at number seven, there's the Professor in the end house there, there's Skin-Lad at number fourteen, he's a fucking nutter. There's all-sorts. Nature is above us, there's moon, there's stars, there's the plough, there's the fucking whatsisname. Moon's coming up full, I feel full, I feel full and cocked and I'll tell you what, stick wi' me tonight, stick wi' Scullery.

The sound of someone whistling is heard. A young man in a suit, **Brink**, *comes across the stage, whistling. Handsome, slow-walking.*

Scullery Hiyah lad.

Brink (*keeps walking*) All right, Scullery?

Scullery Is it Brink?

Brink Aye.

Scullery Have you got a ciggy, lad?

Brink Aye. (*He goes over to him, gives him one.*)

Scullery Aye. Where you off?

Brink Eddie's. (*He lights the cigarette for him.*)

Scullery Eddie's eh?

Brink *starts to walk away.*

Scullery See you.

Brink See you.

Brink *exits.*

Scullery Eddie's eh. Let's have a see.

Blackout.

The lights come up on a room. There is a television up back facing the audience and an old armchair facing the television. **Eddie's Dad** *is in the chair, his back to the audience, fixing a Hoover. The TV is up full, rocketing blast. Front stage, a young lad,* **Eddie**, *topless, is combing his wet hair back to shape it, looking in a mirror on the wall. Knock knock at the door.*

He goes out to answer it and comes in with **Brink***.*

Brink *waves at the man in the chair. The man doesn't look up.* **Brink** *sits at the table near* **Eddie***. He lights up another cigarette.* **Eddie** *carries on. He takes a shirt off the back of the chair and puts it on. He takes it off, angry. He gets an anti-perspirant off the chair, sprays under his arms, still looking in the mirror. Some spray goes over near* **Brink***.* **Brink** *leans right back hands up.* **Eddie** *turns and sprays the head of the man in the armchair.* **Eddie** *puts his shirt on again. He gets his tie off the back of the chair and puts it on, looking in the mirror. Angry again, he takes the tie off. He ties it again.*

Brink Where we goin'?

Eddie (*not looking round, repeats what he thought he heard*) What? Where we goin'?

Brink (*can't hear*) Eh?

Eddie (*exasperated*) Fucking hell. (*He reaches for his aftershave,* – *puts it on.*)

A loud knocking on the wall. **Eddie** *grabs a pan and starts knocking back. The knocking stops.* **Eddie** *does one more knock, then throws the pan down. He puts his jacket on.*

Come on then.

Brink (*doesn't hear*) Eh?

Eddie, *exasperated, just heads for the door.* **Brink** *stubs his fag out and follows.* **Eddie** *holds the door open.* **Brink** *goes out.* **Eddie** *looks at the man in the chair, then goes out, slamming the door.*

The man gets up, turns the TV off, plugs the Hoover in and vacuums in detail the exact spot where **Eddie** *was standing.*

Blackout.

The lights find **Scullery.** *He is sitting high above, bottle in hand. (He's got up there by ladder, rubble, or drain pipe.)*

Scullery Arghhh that lovely smell of the night, my favourite. I sniff it into me blood, sniff (*He does.*) sniff. (*He does.*) Gets me high as a kite.

Brink *and* **Eddie** *pass.*

Scullery All right lads, where you off?

Eddie Pub after pub.

Scullery Well save some birds for me!

Brink Nay, Scullery, the early worm snatches the birds.

They exit.

Scullery Eeee I feel randy me now you know. It's like on the ships when you get it on you yous nowhere to turn.

He sees **Dor** *and* **Lane** *enter – two tarty women.*

Scullery Here you're okay though down the Road, down the alley, the alley alley oh.

Lane *is singing* The Lady is a Tramp.

Scullery *wolf-whistles from above. They look up.*

Dor
Lane } *(together)* SCULLERY!

Scullery Doreen. Lane. Where you off?

Lane Every pub in sight.

Lane *and* **Dor** *laugh.*

Dor What's that?

Scullery Rum.

Dor Give us some.

Scullery Come up here, then.

Dor No way.

Lane *looks up, weighing the distance, grabs* **Dor***'s mouth, opens it and walks her forward.*

Lane Here pour it in, Scullery.

Scullery *leans over, aiming the bottle.*

Up a bit, stop. Left a bit. Stop. Down a bit, stop. Pour.

He does. It goes all over her face. **Lane** *and* **Scullery** *have a good laugh.*

Scullery Come up!

Lane I'm going up me. (*She does.*)

Dor Hang on then.

They set off up.

(*Pulling her skirt in, to the audience.*) Don't look.

Lane *gets up first, sits beside* **Scullery.**

Scullery What a view!

Dor Eh! Oh I thought you meant up me gusset. (*She clambers down beside them.*)

Scullery No, the ROAD.

Lane To me it's like . . . What's that thing you have int' Gents?

Dor Trough.

Lane Thanks Doreen. It's like a long pissie troff to me.

Scullery (*lifting his coat sides for them*) Anyway get stuck in girls wherever you want.

Dor No way, I've just scrubbed me nails.

Lane (*taking the bottle, reading*) Navy rum. You were at sea once weren't you, Scullery?

Scullery Aye aye the big ships.

Lane I thought you had the twang of the sea.

Dor Shiver me timbers.

Lane Come on let's hoist the riggin'.

She jumps on him, they kiss.

Skin-Lad *comes running on.*

Dor Oooh eh look here!

They come up from the kiss.

Skin-Lad *passes.*

Dor
Lane } (*together*) Whoooooooooooooooooooooo.

Scullery SKIN-LAD!

Scullery
Dor } (*together*) He's a fucking nutter!
Lane

They all laugh. **Scullery** *grabs* **Lane** *again for more. They kiss on.* **Dor** *decides to get down and go.*

Dor See you in *Millstone* later, Lane.

Lane (*still snogging, muffled*) See you, Dor.

Dor (*mumbling as she goes*) Snog anything she will. Captain fucking Pugwash.

Dor *exits.*

Scullery *and* **Lane** *come up for air.*

Lane Where'd you get that devil kiss?

Scullery The tropics.

Lane Oooooooooooh take me round world snog by snog start wi' France.

They kiss. Blackout.

Silence. Then some sounds of Road. The sound of a window opening, a voice at breaking point: 'Fucking fuck!' – the window closes. Silence. A dog starts barking. It stops. From somewhere else, the sound of someone crying. It stops. Silence. The lights come up on a little room: sink, table and chair, cooker. An old woman in overcoat and slippers is there. She is emptying a bucket down the sink. She goes and sits at the table.

Molly Dreamy dreamy dreamy dream tu ti tum tum tum tum tum.

On the table is a box full of old make-up. She starts putting lipstick on her frail lips, looking in a little mirror.

Bit o' red. (*She looks in the mirror.*) Bit more o' red. (*She gets up, goes and fills the kettle.*) I'll have some tea in between. (*She starts filling the kettle. She looks out dreaming. The kettle overflows. She stops.*) Oh oh. Imagine that. (*She pours the water away, and puts the kettle on the cooker.*) Dreamy dreamy dream dreamy. (*She lights the gas.*) Dreamy dolly day dream. Where was we. (*She looks round, lost. She goes back and puts a teabag in a cup. She stands waiting for the kettle to boil. She sings.*) Here's me in me likkle house, havin' some tea in between, in between dolling up for a drink, a drink, a drink, I'm standing by me sink. Here's likkle me.

The kettle boils. She puts her hand in her coat cuff and pulls the kettle off. She pours it into the cup. She looks round.

No milk you silly dilk, no sugar you daft likkle bugger. (*She goes back to the table with the teacup. She looks back, sees something below the sink.*) There's milk you silly dilk, you looks round, some is found. Do a little twinkle dance. (*She does a little shuffling dance step as she goes over to it. She picks up the cat's saucer and pours a drop of milk from it into her cup. She puts the saucer down and sits. She starts again on her make-up. She takes an eyebrow pencil out of the box, and looks in the mirror.*) Old eyebrows. (*She starts drawing over her eyebrows.*) Good thing you're a good drawer. You can get round the curves wid your fancy hands. (*She stops, looks up.*) He could, that bust-squeezer. He pushed them from the top down this-away. He see'd me through half the war that man. Stroking, silent, never speaking. Did he die? (*She reaches out.*) I can't see his face. (*She hits her temple.*) I need a new aerial. (*She takes a sip of her tea.*) Dreamy one, likkle me, doll dream. (*She carries on. She comes to powder.*) Powder up. (*She puts powder on a puff.*) Alli-up. (*She puts it on her face. It all scatters. She coughs.*) Puts me in mind of Kenny, Kenny Howcroft the homo. With his big white handbag. A sweet 'un. We used to drink gin off each other's fingers down the bar. (*She looks up.*) Naughty nincompoops. (*She sips her tea, crinkles her nose.*) I used to crinkle my nose like this. (*She crinkles her nose. Starts on her hair, gets a brush and combs a strand up.*) Go up hair, up up. Come on now. Go as I say. Curly curly wurly crackle. My mother used to do it hundred times before bed. Long, white it was. (*Looking out, she goes down with her hand as though touching it. She puts her hand lightly at her throat, looking out for a long time. Pause. Still looking. Silence. Still looking. She takes her teacup, sips.*) Tea's coldish. (*She shivers.*) There's a chill in the air. (*She looks out again. Pause.*) I'll git meself ready and turn out. (*She picks up the little mirror and carries on.*)

Blackout.

The lights come up on the Road.

Professor *appears (among the audience or on stage), glasses crooked and falling off, scruffy old clothes. He carries a long cardboard box under his arm full of papers, and an old, little, battered, portable cassette tape recorder.*

Professor (*to someone in the audience*) I'm the Professor me. I'm not really a professor, I'm just a nosy bastard who wants

to try everything. When I got made redundant I decided to
do an anthropological study of 'Road' and go down in
history. So I moved in the end house here. But all I did was
go down. I lost me wife, me family, half me stomach,
everything. Now all I got left is this tape, and this box full of
all me records, all I could write really. Long ago I gived up
the idea of making a book, and instead, now I just give 'em
out to people for the price of a pint or chips. (*He plucks out a
piece of paper from the box, clears his throat, then reads the title.*)
'Social Life in Road: Wood Street Drinking Club. An
episode that occurred in winter of our Lord nineteen eighty-
two. I went in. A woman was crapping behind the piano.
Two men were fighting over a pie. A row of old prostitutes
were sitting there, still made up as in war years. Price tags
on the soles of their shoes which they kick up at you as you
walk by. I chose the three pounds thirty-two one and bent
her over the billiard table in the back room. Nobody saw. I
could tell she didn't like it so I spoke to her afterwards. She
said she had to do it to keep her four kids decent. I told her
three pounds thirty-two wasn't much, she said she wasn't
much and come to that neither was I. That's where we left
it.' See how easy you can slip when yous a scientist in the
slums.

Lane *has entered earlier and has been listening from a distance.*

Lane Prof!

Professor (*seeing her*) Lane love.

They embrace.

Lane I'll give you one on Wood Street.

He gets the tape recorder out, turns it on, holds the mike out.

Piano, you got splinters if you put your hand on it. Walls,
spit yellow. Tables, soaked in beer. The club. The people.
There was Slack-mouth, Wriggle.

Professor Donny.

Lane Mrs Walmsley.

Professor P.H. Pye.

Lane Oh aye. Face like a throat.

Professor Lake Walter.

Lane What a drinker.

Professor Nelly.

Lane Oh aye Nelly. Sixty-eight years old and still on the game. But she had that senile habit of wantin' sex on the cobbles. Well, when a man walked in wi' no knees you knew he'd been up Nelly.

Professor (*into the mike*) Memories of Wood Street.

Lane It were a bad bastard day when they closed it. My friend slashed on the town hall steps in protest. But it were done with. Put us all int' doldrums.

Professor You mention dole there. I'll give you one from my dole records. (*He takes a piece of paper out, clears his throat, reads.*) 'Study of Unemployment in Road. Bill, forty-two: "You wake up, you look out from under. There's nowhere to go. Your wife's up, she can't sleep, she's counting and pinching pennies all night. My kids are int' next room in old jumble-sale pyjamas. What the fucking hell's happening to me?" Larry, twenty-eight: "You get depressed. It's like black water droppin'. You feel it in the chest."'

Lane You morbid bastard. Life's a spree, Prof. Me and Dor we get our mouth round life and have a chew. Sometimes there's nowt, sometimes it's sloppy, but we keep on snoggin' through. (*She slaps his cheeks.*) See you later, Prof.

Lane *exits.*

Chantal *walks on singing a little child's song. She comes across* **Scullery**.

The **Professor** *watches.*

Chantal Scullery, got a light?

Scullery What's it worth?

Chantal *holds two fags up, one for him. He takes a cig, then lights hers.*

Chantal (*looking at the lighter*) Where'd you get that?

Scullery Spoils of war, my dear hearty.

Chantal Ummmmmmmmmmmmmmmm.

She sets off. Suddenly the cardboard box goes skidding across the stage, and stops in front of her. She stops, looks at it. The **Professor** *speedily wobbles over, stooping, almost sitting on the box.*

Professor Excuse me, my dear, is there any way, well . . .?

She smiles, walks off singing the little child's song. He follows, dragging his cardboard box by its loose string.

Scullery *draws on his fag. The sound of a window opening, and of the 'Dynasty' theme tune on TV inside. Something hits the ground near* **Scullery**, *the window closes,* **Scullery** *picks it up, it's a piece of paper; he unfolds it.*

Scullery (*reads*) 'Dear Scullery, you remind me of a famous star but I can't think of his name. Also you are sex mad. You can come up after if you want. When he's gone out. Also have a wash. Love, Girly. PS. This paper is well-snogged.' (*He looks out to the audience. He screws up the piece of paper and drops it down his pants.*)

Blackout.

The lights come up on a young man sitting on a wooden chair. A bare light bulb is dangling. He is chanting the sound 'Om'.

Skin-Lad Ommmmmmmmmmmmmmmmmmmmmmmm.
He opens his eyes. He sees you. He wants to tell you the story. He feels the need to drift back on the tide of his memory, back, back, back. And I'm the lonely skinhead again. Jogging away, everyday, to be the best, to be the best. And the press-ups. And the sit-ups. And the one-two-three, one-two-three, one-two-three, one-two-three. And you've gotta be fit to fight, and I do every Saturday night, with my friends at weekends, fight. Do you know about fighting? No. I'll tell you in my story. And I want to be the best skinhead and I want to give everything, every single thing, to the experience of the tingle. I'll tell you about the tingle later.

And you've gotta be fit to fight, and practise tactics every
night. (*He practises on imaginary opponent.*) Do you? I do.
(*Practises.*) Do you work in the asphalt factory? I did.
(*Practises, stops.*) I'll explain. (*He indicates imaginary opponent.*)
My opponent! Anyone you like. City fan, the cunt that
shagged Ricky's bird, Ted the foreman. You choose. Targets!
(*Indicates down imaginary body.*) Face, neck, beerbag, dick,
shin, top of the foot. Top of the foot. Today I want the
neck, this vein here. I don't want to fuck Christine Dawson,
I don't want my mother's love, I don't want to work at the
engineering firm, I want the neck, this vein here. (*Practises.*)
Tactics, new techniques. What does he think? What do you
think? (*Strikes.*) The neck and that's that. He thought, you
thought, the neck and that is that. Now I've told you about
the three things you need to get to the experience of the
tingle. One fitness, told you. Two, tactics, told you. Three,
new techniques, I told you. Now I'll tell you about the tingle.
(*He comes offstage and into the audience.*) Well it's . . . You can't
say it can you? . . . It'll come when you're fighting.
Sometimes in the middle, sometime beginning, sometime
end, but it won't stay . . . it's like you are there, you are
fighting, but 'you' are not there . . . (*Pause.*) You don't
understand. (*Pause.*) Anyway, once you've had it, you need
it, and I thought that's all there was until that night, right,
should I tell you about that night? No. I'll show you. (*He
leaps back onstage.*) I came out the disco, last man to leave, all
my lads had gone. I'd been talking to Mickey Isherwood the
bouncer. 'See you Jim.' 'Aye, see you Ishey.' Then I saw
them. Skins. Bolton boot boys. Skinheads. Some sitting on
the wall. Some standing. I moved off to the right. 'Eh,
cunty.' 'Eh, git head.' 'Come 'ere.' I looked at the moon. I
heard the crack of denim, the scuffle down the wall, the pad
and fall of the Dr Martins, pad, pad, pad. I closed my eyes.
Pad, pad. As they moved in, pad, pad, I moved out. Pad,
pad. I felt their breath . . . (*Loud cry.*) KIYAA! . . . lifted one
man by the chin . . . can you imagine it? Magnificent . . .
they were scattering. Caught one man between thigh and
calf, took him round to the ground, fingers up the nose
dragged a pace, nutted, lifted my fingers to pierce out his
eyes when to my surprise I saw a figure watching, like a

ghost, all pale in the night. Seemed like I'd known him all
my life. He was laughing at me. Mocking my whole fucking
life. I sprang, when I arrived he'd gone. Too quick for me.
No, I saw him disappear down a blind alley. I had him now.
I had him now! He was facing the wall in a sort of peeing
position. I moved in to strike, my fist was like a golden orb
in the wet night, I said it was night, I struck deep and
dangerous and beautiful with a twist of the fist on the out.
But he was only smiling, and he opened his eyes to me like
two diamonds in the night. I said it was night, and said
'Over to you Buddha'. (*Pause.*) So now I just read the
dharma. And when men at work pass the pornography, I
pass it on and continue with the dharma. And when my
mother makes egg and bacon and chips for me I push it
away towards the salt cellar and read of the dharma. And
when the man on the bus push I continue with the dharma.
Ommmmmmmmm.

Blackout.

The Road.

Scullery *looks up to one of the windows above him. It has sacking
hanging and looks deserted.*

Scullery See this derelict house here? (*He takes a pillow-case
out of his pocket and starts unfolding it.*) I've been meaning to
give it a ransacking, see if there's any coppers to be made.
You never know. (*He clambers up to the window.*)

As **Scullery** *gets in,* **Brenda** *comes on.*

Brenda Scullery.

Scullery Brenda. Where's that juicy daughter of yours?

Brenda Don't mention muck to me. Eh, Scullery do you
remember the alley wall, me and you, what a night. I went
home with bits of brick in me bum.

Scullery Aye well that was sometime ago Brenda, before
you flopped.

Brenda Scullery, that night I felt I'd bin shot. (*She reaches up.*)

Scullery Really?

Brenda Really. (*Up on her toes.*)

Scullery (*reaching down*) Juliet.

Brenda (*jumping up*) Romeo.

He gets her arm, pulls her up a bit.

You're the only man.

He gets her higher towards him.

The only one.

Their faces nearly touching.

Lend us a fiver.

He drops her.

Scullery Flea Queen!

Brenda Up yours!

Scullery Come on get in me sack I'll weigh you in as rags!

Brenda (*going*) Aw fuck off!

Scullery Get tidy!

Brenda Piss off!

Brenda *exits.*

Scullery (*to the audience*) Some ladies. (*He goes into the house again. From inside.*) What a mess and pong.

We hear him rummaging. He comes to the window, leans on the sill.

How is it when, tell me this, when you goes in an auld empty house there's always an old doll, (*He holds up a doll.*) burnt paper, (*He holds up a bit of burnt newspaper, looking at it.*) and a Christmas card. (*He holds it up and lets it drop to the street.*)

He goes back in. He comments on what he sees and what it's worth.

Right get picking the Road's bones. Old tap 30p. (*He drops it in the sack.*) Basket, a bob. (*He drops it in.*) Bit o' copper piping, one pound seventy. Crucifix. (*He looks at it closely.*) They're no good without a Jesus. (*He chucks it.*) A musical box! (*He picks up a little, dirty, kid's plastic musical box.*) I'm having that. (*He shoves it in his special pocket. He comes out, throws the full pillow-case down to the street and clambers over the sill. As he's bringing his leg over.*) Might have this bit of sack here. You never know. (*He rips it down and he drops to the ground. He starts stuffing the sacking into the pillow-case.*)

Suddenly a big bald man appears at the same window, angry.

Bald What the bloody hell's goin' on!

Scullery *looks out to the audience. He looks slowly up to* **Bald**.

Scullery Sorry, I thought there was no one living there.

Bald Well there bloody well is.

A woman's voice is heard from back in the house.

Mrs Bald What's up?

Bald Nowt. Just bin' robbed.

Mrs Bald Well kick him.

Bald I'll kick you in a minute. (*He turns to* **Scullery**.) Here. Give us that.

Scullery (*slowly, reluctantly, passing the bag back*) Sorry.

Bald *snatches it.* **Scullery** *passes up the Christmas card.*

Bald I don't want that.

Bald *goes in.*

Mrs Bald (*off, inside*) Are you coming back to bed?

Bald (*off, inside*) Shut it.

Scullery *looks out to the audience in disbelief.*

Blackout.

The lights come up on an old armchair, ironing-board and iron. A man is polishing his shoes. The man is middle-aged, soft-spoken, threadbare, with a big hole in his sock.

Jerry   I can't get over it. I can't get over the past, how it was. I just can't. (*He puts his shoes down.*) Oh God, I get these strong feelings inside and they're so sad I can hardly stand it. (*He puts his tie on the ironing board, irons it.*) Oh, oh I can feel one now, it's breaking my heart with its strength and tears are coming in my eyes, and that's just because I thought of something from ago. Oh God. (*He gets down to ironing again.*) Oh they were lovely lovely times though, and such a lilt to them, I go down it when I think. (*He sits down, looking up.*) I hate to mention it, but that big silver ball turning there and all the lights coming off it onto us lot dancing below, and the big band there. And all the lads and girls I knew, all with their own special character. And the way you stood, you know, and you had a cigarette. You even lit a cigarette different then. There was some way, I can't do it now, good thing too, if I could I'd cry me flipping heart out. That's why I never wear Brylcream these days. I can't. National service too, you did. Everybody did it. You never complained much then, you never felt like complainin', I don't know why. National service though, you'd all be there. I was RAF, in that soft blue uniform, beret. (*He touches his head.*) When you had a break you'd lie on your bunk, your mate might say, 'Give us a tab'. (*He puts his hands over his eyes.*) And when you went on leave home. To your home town. The weather always seemed to be a bit misty and you'd be walking around familiar streets in your uniform. And everyone would have a little something to say to you. And you'd go to your girlfriend's factory. And they'd send up for her: 'There's a man in uniform to see you.' And you'd wait outside, take your cigs out your top pocket. (*He touches there.*) Light up. Stand there in the misty weather, in your blue uniform. Full up with something. And everyone was an apprentice something. Serving your time. Or you could work for more money in the beginning in a warehouse or the railway, but it didn't pay off eventually. Or be a fly-boy and sell toys and annuals in the pubs. There was so many jobs then. A lot of people would start one in the

morning, finish it, start another in the afternoon, finish it,
and go in somewhere else the next day. You had the hit
parade. Holidays in the Isle of Man or Blackpool. '*Volare*.'
We all felt special but safe at the same time. I don't know.
You know I'm not saying this is right, but girls didn't even
go in pubs. They didn't. At the dance, in the interval the
lads all went in the pub next door. The girls stayed in
the dance hall, then afterwards we all came back. And the
girls, so pretty. Oh when I think of them. (*He puts his hands
over his eyes.*) And you went courting in them days. You
courted. You walked with them and they had their cardigan
over their arm. (*He puts his hand up to his face.*) And the
pictures. You went twice, three times a week. The stars, the
music, black and white, the kissing. Sex. When I say the
word now, and when I said it then it feels different in me.
I know it sounds, you know, but it does. I can't get away
from the past. I just can't. But no matter what they say.
I can't see how that time could turn into this time. So
horrible for me and so complicated for me. And being poor
and no good, no use. (*He looks up, tears in his eyes.*) I see 'em
now me old friends, their young faces turning round and
smiling. Fucking hell who's spoiling life, me, us, them or
God?

Blackout.

*The sound of a dustbin-lid falling down and shouting. The lights
come up on the Road.*

Scullery *and* **Blowpipe** *burst in.* **Blowpipe** *is banging an empty
beer crate on the floor and all about.*

Scullery It's wrong! It's all fucking wrong! (*He shouts to the
sky.*) You fucking bastards!

Blowpipe *flops out.* **Scullery** *kicks a dustbin flying.*

Scullery (*to* **Blowpipe**) That's me! (*To the audience.*) That's
me!

Blowpipe *has picked up the dustbin lid and is banging it on the
floor like a warrior.* **Scullery** *rips his coat off and faces the
audience.*

Scullery Come on one at a time! I walk tall.

He turns away, stares at **Blowpipe.** **Blowpipe** *stops the banging.*
Scullery *goes and stands facing the wall. Silence. Then he turns to*
the audience and bursts out laughing.

Scullery Sorry about that mates. You've got to clear the
system once in a while an't you? Ha! Come on Blowpipe. (*He*
starts dusting him off.) Smarten yourself up. Got get in for
another pint soon.

Clare *comes on, a young girl about 16.*

Clare Hello Scullery.

Scullery Hello Clare love. Where you goin'?

Clare To see Joey.

Scullery Oh aye.

Clare He's still not eating Scullery. Nowt for four days now.

Scullery Nowt? Not even a pie?

Clare No.

Scullery Bloody hell!

Clare I'm worried sick. What can I say to him, Scullery?

Scullery Fish, chips, pudding and peas.

Clare Scullery!

Scullery *has a good laugh.*

Clare *exits.*

Molly *enters.*

Scullery (*seeing her*) Auld Molly. Gi' us a song.

Molly Gi' us a drink.

Scullery Blowpipe!

Blowpipe *gives her the bottle. She has a swig.* **Blowpipe** *tries to*
retrieve it. **Scullery** *knocks him down.*

Scullery Get back.

Molly *has finished her drink.*

Molly Reet. What do you want?

Scullery Owt.

Molly I'll sing you what I sang at one o' me weddings.

Molly *sings a beautiful old Lancashire folk song. She finishes.*
Blowpipe *is moved. The lights dim.* **Molly** *comforts him.*

Molly *and* **Blowpipe** *go off.*

At the same time **Scullery** *wheels a bed out from the shadows. He pushes it centre and into a spotlight. In the bed is a young lad of about 17.* **Scullery** *stands behind the bed-head and states strongly:*

Scullery 'JOEY'S STORY.'

He goes off.

Darkness. A loud knocking starts. The knocking stops. Silence.

Mother's voice (*off*) Joey come out! Come on out for
Godsake. JOEY!!

Silence. The lights come up. **Joey** *is curled up in bed staring out.*

Joey I'm not lonely. I'm lying here now for four days. She
keeps on trying to bring food in. I won't have none. I'm not
to eat or drink. I'm on a diet since Wednesday. AND NO
ONE'S GONNA STOP ME!!

Pause.

They keep on a-knocking, keep on a-banging on the bastard
door. But I won't answer. Because what's out there anyroad
eh? They might as well put a sign over the door top here
reading 'Gents'. Because out there is just a bog. The world's
a fat toilet. It's true that, true as breath that little comment.
True as trees . . . Fuck me, you babble when you've not
eaten don't you? They're always a-falling out, your thoughts.
You get a great brainful then your mouth sicks them out.
This is what I'm seeking though. I want everything right
out. Right the way out. This is why I'm on the diet. Fuck me
I'm dry. My throat's a bone. (*He looks all around him.*)

Fucking hell am I in a film or what? (*He laughs to himself.*)
Madhouse in' it this nineteen eighty-seven. Packed with
muck. There's no jobs. I was robbed of mine. My future
snatched. A smash and grab job. I don't care now though.
Bloody hell I'm knacked.

A loud knock on the door.

Father's voice (*off*) Clare's here. Do you want to see her or
not?!

Joey Get stuffed.

Father's voice (*off*) You bloody little nutter!

Clare (*off*) No, Mr Cragg let me go in.

The door is unlocked. He goes right down under the blankets.

Clare *comes in and closes the door.*

Joey.

No reply.

Joey, come on love.

No reply.

Joey.

*She goes over to touch him. He does a monkey impersonation. She
screams.*

Joey! What you doing?

Joey Nothing.

Clare Oh Joey, this isn't right. Why are you starving
yourself? What's it for, everybody's worried sick for you.
You can't just do this you know.

Joey Why not?

Clare Look we all feel like this sometime. But life must go
on.

Joey Why?

Clare Eh? Oh don't be stupid. What about me, I've no job

now either but I'm not behaving like a bloody big kid.
Anyone can do that you know.

Joey Look if I'd wanted Marje Proops I would have writ' to
the bitch. GO HOME!

Pause.

Clare (*soft*) Joe.

Joey Can't you see this is something else, eh? Go on, get
out.

Silence. Long pause.

Clare I'd rather get in bed.

*Silence. He looks at her. She takes her coat off. Then her top, then
her skirt and gets in bed with him. He just keeps watching.*

Blackout.

*At this point, either a blackout then lights up to denote time passing,
or the following speech:*

Bisto, *the pub DJ, enters with a pack of leaflets. (On them is
something like, 'Bisto and his Beatoven disco. Tonight at the
Millstone Pub'.) He throws these out to the audience as he speaks.
He wears a hat with two stuffed fingers on top in the V-sign.*

Bisto How you doing? Okey dokey? I hopey so. I'm Bisto
the foul mouthiest DJ you'll ever know. (*Catchphrase, he
shoves two fingers up.*) You'll get used to me. (*He points.*) You'd
better. Ha! When you've done here, why not come down to
Millstone Pub and move up and down wi' BISTO and his
BEATOVEN disco. (*He shoves two fingers up.*) You'll get used
to me. (*He points.*) You'd better. I'm available for weddings,
engagements, barmitzvahs, anything you like. I guarantee to
get the most miserable cunt at the wedding up and dancing
or your money back. You'll get used to me. You'd better.

He exits.

The lights come up. **Joey** *and* **Clare** *are sitting up in bed.*

Joey I said go home.

Clare No I'm staying with you. Anything you can do I can do better.

Joey (*pleased, yodelling*) OOOOOOOOOHHHHhhhhhh!

Clare Are we protesting?

Joey I don't know love. Why are you here anyway?

Clare I don't know. I suppose I don't know what else to do. Every day's the same now. You were my only hobby really, now you're out of it, seems mad to carry on, all me ambition's gone. I filled in a *Honey* quiz last week. 'Have you got driving force?' I got top marks all round. But where can I drive it Joe? I lost my lovely little job. My office job. I bloody loved going in there you know. Well you do know, I told you about it every night. I felt so sweet and neat in there. Making order out of things. Being skilful. Tackling an awkward situation here and there. To have a destination. The bus stop, then the office, then the work on the desk. Exercise to my body, my imagination, my general knowledge. Learning life's little steps. Now I'm saggy from tip to toe. Every day's like swimming in ache. I can't stand wearing the same clothes again and again. Re-hemming, stitching, I'm sick with it, Joe. I heard my mum cry again last night. My room's cold. I can't buy my favourite shampoo. Everybody's poor and sickly-white. Oh Joe! Joe! Joe!

Joey (*comforting her*) Never mind lovey. Never mind.

Clare Oh Joe I want to understand. Are we protesting?

Joey No, we're just . . .

Clare Eh?

Joey Seeing what will take place in our heads.

Clare But we might die.

Joey We might not. We might have some secret revealed to us.

Clare Oh Joe.

Mother's voice (*from outside*) Your mum's on the phone Clare. She's worried, when are you going home?

No reply.

Clare.

Clare Tell her I'm on an adventure and not to worry!

Joey (*pleased*) Oh yes. (*He yodels.*)
OOOOOOOOOOOOHhhhhhhhhhhhhh! (*He kisses her.*)

Mother's voice (*off*) Oh Clare. Oh.

She goes away. The sound of her going down steps.

Clare I've never been so happy as the day we met you know.

Joey Go on. It was good though wun't it. I remember you pulled your T-shirt down a bit to show me your tan.

Clare Oh yeah I did.

Joey You were a right flirt then wun't you?

Clare No! That was the first time I'd ever done owt so brave.

Joey Yeah maybe, but you'd had it before 'an't you?

Clare Only once. With Gary Stones. On his couch when his mum was ill upstairs. I didn't like it much.

Joey I'm not surprised.

Clare What do you mean?

Joey He's like bad beef that bloke.

Clare Is he heck.

Joey Oh well go and have a pigging scene with him then!

Clare Oh.

Silence.

What about you then. You've had more than a few sexual whatsisnames before me, sexual adventures shall we say. According to what I've heard anyroad. What about her then,

Jackie Snook. She's no starlet is she, more like a fartlet . . .
Looks like God give her an extra armpit to use as a mouth.

Joey Shut it.

Clare Uh.

Silence.

Eh Joe, serious though, tell me about your first sex. You
never have.

Joey Why?

Clare I told you.

No reply.

Now we're together in this we should bring everything out.

Joey Well this is what I'm trying to do get everything out.

Clare Come on then.

Joey Yeah. Right then. Okay, I was . . . I thought I'd told
you this.

Clare No.

Joey Okay. Me and Steve Carlisle went to the Nevada in
Bolton, roller skating, Thursday night, 'The brothel on
wheels'. I was about fourteen then. We was pretending to be
French, talking to birds in the accent. This girl was next to
me an' I said "Ello you are verrrry beootiful.' She said
'You're not French you.' I said 'I ham, I ham.' Anyway I
kept it up for about fifteen minutes, then admitted it wun't
true, took her over the park and fucked her up against a
bulldozer wheel.

Clare Oh. And what was it like?

Joey Very muddy.

Clare Uh.

Joey Are you jealous now?

Clare Am I heck.

Joey *gives a gentle laugh. Pause. Silence.*

Clare (*a thought has just struck her.*) Joe?

Joey Yeah.

Clare This what we're doing, is it 'owt to do with Phil Bott? Phil the Commie. Because he talks so fast I've never understood a word he's said yet. Tell me no.

Joey No.

Pause.

I tried all that for a bit. I went with Phil to his meetings, but still I cun' decide who to attack. There's not one thing to blame. There's not just good and bad, everything's deeper. But I can't get down there to dig out the answer. I try. I try me bestest. I keep plunging meself in me mind but I return empty-handed. I'm unhappy. So fucked off! And every bastard I meet is just the same.

Silence. **Clare** *tries to kiss him. He resists. Pause.*

Clare Joe, I'm getting hungry.

Pause.

Joe.

He pulls the sheet back hard.

Joey Go!

Clare No, Joe. No.

Joey Get out!

Clare No. (*She pulls the covers back up.*)

Joey Well don't start, then.

Pause.

Clare Why we doing this, Joe?

Joey I'm after something.

Clare What?

Joey How should I know? If I knew it I wun't be piggin' after it, would I?

Clare I don't understand you.

Joey Look there's summat missing. Life can't be just this, can it? What everybody's doing.

Clare That way madness lies.

Joey Eh?

Clare That's what my mum says. Any time there's any of that. Any clever talk on the telly she says it to us. She says just get on with it. Live your life and that's all there is to it.

Joey Oh?

Clare Well what does that mean?

Joey You're not serious. You're not even a joke. You're just like all the rest of them. Frightened to sniff the wind for fear it'll blow your brain upside down and then you'll (*He puts on a pathetic voice.*) 'Have to do something different'. Wasting your whole lives. Work, work, work, work, work. Small wages, small wages, small wages. Gettin' by with a smile. Gettin' by without a smile. Work, work, work, work. Small wages. Then death with the big 'D'. Not even a smell left over from it all. If you're lucky, a see-through memory, slowly dissolving like 'Steradent'.

Clare Don't insult my mum you!

Joey OH FOR FUCK'S SAKE, IS THAT ALL YOU CAN SAY?

Clare (*seeing he's out of control, trying to cool him*) Oh Joe. Come on. Bloody hell. I didn't mean nowt.

Joey EH!

Clare (*trying again*) I'm sorry, Joe. OK. Bloody hell. I mean bloody hell. Come on Joe. I didn't mean nowt when I said it. I mean this is not like you Joe.

Joey (*anger rising again*) UH.

Clare Now don't start, Joe. What I mean is you must admit you've not shown me this face before. I had no idea.

Joey (*coming round, a bit embarrassed*) Aye well, try having an idea now and again, eh. It don't hurt you know. Try, try it.

Clare (*faked laugh*) Eh, come on now. (*Pause. Silence. A bit afraid, quiet.*) When did you start thinking like this, Joe?

Joey (*quietly*) When did I start!? When did I stop's more like it! What the fuck's it all about Clare?! That's the one, that's the boy, that's putting the head butt on my heart. You don't get the chance to find out. They rush you from the cradle to the grave. But now we've come to a standstill, no job, no hope, you've got to ask the question. You've got to ask. And it does you fucking good, too.

Clare It don't look like it's done you much good. Lying there, half-dead.

Joey Come on love. What the fuck else is worth doing? (*He shoves his face violently at hers.*) EH?!!

She screams. Loud knocking starts on the door.

He pulls her to him and kisses her with love.

Blackout.

They remain in bed onstage. The next scene occurs around them. The lights come up on the Road.

Scullery *is tidying himself up. He's combing his hair in a small mirror.*

Scullery Have a good guess at me age, go on. (*He puts his comb away.*) I'm older than you think. Ha. (*He pulls his jacket together.*) I was just thinking there. How do we go about building a better future for our kiddies.

The **Professor** *enters.*

Professor Scullery, Scullery.

Scullery Prof. Prof.

Professor Can I do a recollection of you?

Scullery Who me? No. Really? Go on then.

The **Professor** *turns the tape on, hands over the mike. The mike makes* **Scullery** *feel like a night-club host.*

Testing, one two, one two. I don't know where to start. I've had a long life, some of it rough skin, some of it smooth. But on the 'hole' I've always gone down. I likes it that way. Thank you very much ladies and gents, thank, thank you. I don't know what else I can say really but bless the dark and all who scrape in her. And if you're driving home tonight give us a lift you tight stink. And just remember folks if God did make them little green apples he also made snot. Thank you. Thank.

He has got the hang of it now and takes up the mike again. The **Professor** *hurriedly retrieves it.*

Well that's worth a drink in' it Prof?

Professor (*putting the tape away*) Er well I . . .

Scullery You can give us a lift for that! Yeearrr. (*He jumps on the* **Professor**'s *back.*)

The **Professor** *runs out.* **Scullery** *riding him.*

Scullery (*laughing*) This is 'Road' for you. This is 'Road'.

He laughs, laughing uproariously, as they exit.

Blackout.

The lights come up on **Joey**'s *room. Two weeks later.*

Joey *is sitting up in bed with his arm around* **Clare**. *She is sleeping.* **Joey**'s *face really shows the strain now, it is taut and white.*

Joey I feel like England's forcing the brain out me head. I'm sick of it. Sick of it all. People reading newspapers: 'EUROVISION LOVERS', 'OUR QUEEN MUM', 'MAGGIE'S TEARS', being fooled again and again. What the fuck-fuck is it? Where am I? Bin lying here two weeks now. On and on through the strain. I wear pain like a hat. Everyone's insane. The world really is a bucket of devil sick. Every little moment's stupid. I'm sick of people – people, stupid people. Frying the air with their mucky words, their mucky thoughts, their mucky deeds. Horrible sex being had under rotten bedding. Sickly sex being had on the waterbed.

Where has man gone? Why is he so wrong? Why am I hurt
all through? Every piece of me is bruised or gnawed raw, if
you could see it, my heart's like an elbow. I've been done
through by them, it, the crushing sky of ignorance, thigh of
pignorance. What did I do! What was my crime? Who do I
blame? God for giving me a spark of vision? Not enough of
one, not enough of the other, just enough for discontent,
enough to have me right out on the edge. Not able to get
anyone out here with me, not able to get in with the rest.
Oh God I'm so far gone it's too late. I'm half dead and I'm
not sad or glad. I'm not sad or glad, what a fucking, bastard,
bitching, cunt state to be in. I'm black inside. Bitterness has
swelled like a mighty black rose inside me. Its petals are
creaking against my chest. I want it out! out! out! Devil,
God, Devil, God, Devil, God, save me something. Anything.
There's got to be summat will come to help us. If only we
can make the right state. If I can only get myself into the
right state. This is it. This is why I'm on the diet. (*He looks
around, remembering.*) Fucking hell am I in a film or what? Or
snot, or what. (*He is tightening.*) IIIIIIIIIIIIIIII bring up
small white birds covered in bile and fat blood, they was my
hopes. I bring up a small hard pig that was my destiny. I'd
like to bring it all out but bbbbbbbbbbbbbut I've gone all
constipated on bitterness, it won't remove itself. God give me
a laxative if you got one. Ha! AArrrrrrgh! Arrrrrgh! Oh
AAArrrrrgh! (*He's sweating and straining.*) Come out, come
out, you tight bastard. Oh no! Death suck me up through
that straw inside my spine! No leave me! Oh I'm full of dark
frost. Who's done this to me! And why? Oh why? Is it worth
that extra bit of business to see me suffer, is it? I blame you
BUSINESS and you RELIGION its favourite friend, hand
in hand YOU HAVE MURDERED THE CHILD IN MAN!
MURDERERS! CUNTS! I'D LIKE TO CUT OPEN YOUR
BELLIES AND SEE THE BROWN POUR!

*It should appear that he's going to get out of bed to really kill
somebody. Then* Clare *wakes. She puts her arm on him.*

Clare Joey.

Joey Eh?

Clare Joey, I feel so faint and white. I can't hardly see my Joey.

Joey Don't worry about it. There might be a message or a sign soon.

Clare Uh?

Joey You never can tell when it's a going to come on you. Fuck me I wish I could sweat or something, I'm like paper.

Clare I'm empty and dried-out too, it's so weird now Joe. (*Silence*.) Joe, is my skin cracking?

Joey No.

Clare Around my mouth at the corners is there any cracking?

Joey (*a quick glance*) No.

Clare It feels like it is. (*She starts to sing to herself, very soft*.) 'Don't know much about history. Don't know much about society. But I do know that I love you and I know if you'd love me too what a wonderful world this would be. What a wonderful world this would be.'

Silence.

I love you so much, Joey.

Joey Eh?

Clare I love you, my man. Perhaps if I cried you could drink up my tears.

Joey Be quiet now.

Clare It feels right funny. I can feel things very fine with my body now. Very fine like the silence within silence within silence. Joey is it death-time?

Joey (*shocked*) Stop it! You're talking now like you've never talked in your life.

Clare Where's it coming from?

Joey You! You!

Clare Who?

Joey Oh no. You're more advanced now than me. You're going somewhere. A state. Into a state.

Clare Eh?

Joey Are you in a trance or what?

Clare I don't know.

Joey Just shout out things. That's how I'll test you. Just say things what come into your head.

Clare How can a? A can't hardly speak.

Joey What do you mean?

Clare I'm so knackered out. A feel I'm just holding on by the threads. One or two fine wet threads, the rest have dried an' broke.

Joey Oh my dear.

Clare Don't worry. I still love you, that's left. I keep on seeing faces, like me dad's, me mum's, me dad's again. I still want to cry when I see me dad's dismantled face. He lost his last job you know. Just think one day there might be the last job on earth. And everyone will come out to see the man lose it. They'll all watch as he comes up to his last hour. The last hooter blow whooooooooooo oh oooooo oooooooooo oooooo I'm being corny now, in't a Joey? Oh my it's white in here behind the eyes, so misty.

She closes her eyes. **Joey** *holds her. He makes a fist. He shakes it at the audience. He shakes it up at the sky. He shakes it at the door where the family are outside. He shakes it down under the bed. Then he puts it in front of his face and bites into his hand.*

Blackout.

The lights come up.

Clare *is lying down one side of the bed. He's covered up her face. He is now the other way round, lying with his feet on the pillow, his head hanging over the edge. He sees the audience upside down, his* *eyes staring up, his mouth wide open. He makes a noise in his throat.*

Joey Gaaaaaraaaaaaa ga gaaaaaaaarr gaaaa aaaaaaaa. Ga. Ga. Agraaaaaaaaa ga. Gaaaaaaaaaaaaa aaa. Ga ga. Smart in' it? Smart arse in' it? To end back to front on the bed. Look at me. I am pain. I am now from tip to toe. Look at me I am the solution. There is no solution. How about that then. That's the smart-arsest simplest answer going. The last answer to the first question. There is no solution. (*He stops and stares.*) But you're all adding a 'maybe' aren't you. (*He winks then dies.*)

From out of the shadows **Scullery** *comes over. He takes the sheet and covers* **Joey**'s *face.*

Scullery (*to the audience*) Hey, we's gonna miss last orders. I's have to see Girly, then I'll get in there with you. I'll just step back into the dark. (*He starts stepping back.*) See you soon.

The lights fade to blackout.

Interval

Two scenes run at the same time: disco in the theatre, pub in the bar. The bar scene begins later and ends earlier to give people time to get in and out and return to the disco for the floor show. Acts in the pub can be anything the actors choose.

The Disco.

After the blackout at the end of Act One, the lights come up a little. A pause to establish the interval. Then a burst of light and music. The stage has become a disco, up behind a flashing record deck is **Bisto**.

Bisto Welcome to *Millstone Pub*. I'm Bisto. And this is the Beatoven Disco. You'll get used to me . . . You'd better. By my calculators we've only got fifteen minutes till last orders, so let's dance!

Madonna or any full dance sound up to full. After a minute, if enough people don't go through to the bar, Madonna down to half, under.

I've just had a call through from the bar saying where the fuck is everybody. There's a turn coming on in a minute, so go and drink or stay and dance.

Madonna up to full. Madonna into the Bee Gees' Saturday Night Fever *under the intro.*

Come on, the floor is yours, so grab a mug and cut the rug, take your feet and mash the beat, slide out there and show some flare, in other words, dance you buggers!

Bee Gees up to full. Bee Gees fade under.

Ah the Bee Gees, great bunch of lads. Right. Have we any rockers in tonight, aye rock and roll. Now I defy any bastard not to dance to this next delight . . . the Teddy Boys' treat . . . a fifties' classic . . . 'RED HOT BOLLOCKS' . . . oh sorry . . . 'GREAT BALLS OF FIRE!!!!'

Great Balls of Fire (Jerry Lee Lewis) comes straight in. When it ends.

That's what you can expect from Bisto. Music to dance to,

talk through, an' grab a slag to. All your favourite tunes an' flashing fucking lights an' all. This next one is one o' me personal favourites, and I dedicate it to . . . well you know who you are, ya bitch!

Can't Get Used to Losing You (Andy Williams) fades up to full.

Meanwhile, in the bar . . .

Once a fair amount of audience are in, the compère, **Tom Stanley***, gets onstage.*

Tom Stanley Ladies and gents, ladies and gents, can we have a bit of hush an' order for a sec. Thank you. As you know, tonight is turn night here in the old *Millstone Pub*, and we've got someone really special in tonight. I'm sure you'll join me in welcoming Chance Peterson ladies and gents. Chance. Thank you.

Chance *comes on. He stands onstage, guitar round neck, sings a bit, then collapses against the back wall.*

Tom Stanley I must apologize for this, ladies and gents. That's the last fucking time we'll have him. In a way, it's dropped us in the muck. Anyway, er. I know. I know. Anyone in the audience like to come up here on our famous stage an' give us a song or summat? (*He peers out.*) Is there anybody out there? Ha.

Scullery *steps forward and onstage.*

Tom Stanley Scullery!

Scullery *sings to a taped accompaniment.*

Tom Stanley *returns.*

Tom Stanley Thank you ladies an' gents, could I ask you all to drink up now as last orders is gone. I don't mean to be unkindly. But shut up, sup up and shove off. May I say if you rush it you might catch the erotic dancers in our disco room.

Meanwhile, in the disco . . .

Can't Get Used to Losing You *(Andy Williams) plays, ends.*

Bisto Right now. We have a special thrill for you tonight. We've got live entertainment, when I say live I mean wild, when I say wild I mean red hot, when I say red hot I mean a right fucking turn on. That TITilating Trio, the exotic, erotic, you'll never believe your eyes, or their thighs, the breast in the land – THE ELECTRIC CLUTCH! THAT'S SHEENA . . .

She runs on.

That's TINA . . .

She runs on.

That's MAUREENA.

She runs on.

This is sex.

They dance. It goes wrong – one of the girls does her back in. The others carry her off.

What a fuck up, and I thought we were in for a bit of minge as well. Never mind. Right now it's time for the last song of the evening. It's a smooch, and as is customary at this time, Bisto asks you to glance around the room. There must be someone out there you've seen tonight and thought should I, could I. Well you can. Go on. Go over, take his or her hand, and just dance yourselves together. Beautiful. I want to thank each and every one of you for coming down tonight, and just remember. I love you, we love you, so you love you too, you're worth it, people. *(Soft and slow.)* You'll get used to me. You'd better.

Je t'aime *(Jane Birkin) up to full.*

Scullery *gets people from the audience up onstage to dance together.* **Bisto** *comes down to help.* **Lane** *and* **Dor** *come in and get partners up. A drunken young* **Soldier** *comes onstage. Standing, wobbling, holding a woman's coat and bag.* **Helen** *(middle-aged woman) comes through the crowd to find him; takes her coat and bag, leads him off. The dance continues until the record ends.*

Act Two

A spotlight picks out **Scullery** *above. He puts his music box on. It plays* When You Wish Upon a Star. *He dances to it. It finishes. He exits.*

The lights come up as a chip shop opens in the corner, **Manfred** *the owner, and his assistant, a* **Scotch Girl**.

Dor *and* **Lane** *go over.*

Manfred What you havin' girls?

Lane Whooo don't ask her that.

Dor Have you got a sausage.

Lane *laughs.*

Dor Serve it up love.

Scotch Girl Do you want chips?

Lane Aye the noo.

Dor She's Scottchish.

Lane I know.

Dor Any haggis there?

While **Dor** *and* **Lane** *are paying the girl . . .*

Helen *and the* **Soldier** *come up.*

Helen Two please. Chips and fish and pudding and chips. Gravy please. (*She sees the girl. She moves the* **Soldier** *to the other side.*)

Helen *and the* **Soldier** *exit after buying their chips.*

Manfred (*to the audience*) Come on now. CHIPS. FISH. MUSHY PEAS. PUDDING. SPECIALS. MEAT PIES. CHEESE AND ONION PIES. SAUSAGE BATTERED OR NOT. BURGER. CHICKEN. BLACK PUDDING. FISHCAKE. BARM CAKES.

Scotch Girl (*shouts to him*) The vans haven't come!

Manfred Oh. LADIES AND GENTS WE'VE GOT CHIPS.
LOADS OF CHIPS. LONG CHIPS. SHORT CHIPS. CHIP
CHIPS. COME AN' GET 'EM WHILE THEY'RE HOT
BLEEDING CHIPS. (*To the girl.*) Fucking hell. It would
happen tonight when we's got a road full. I could a made
me bastard fortune tonight. COME ON LOVE. CHIPS ARE
HERE. THE LOVELIEST IN THE LAND. (*He holds one
up.*) LOOK AT THAT NORTHERN BEAUTY. IT'S THE
LENGTH AND THE DEPTH AND THE LACK OF
GREASE THAT MAKES IT WHAT IT IS. (*He swallows it.*)
WHAT A VINTAGE. DON'T MISS THEM LOVE. COME
AND BUY , . .

The lights cross-fade to . . .

Dor *and* **Lane** *appear high up eating chips.*

Lane It were packed in there tonight weren't it?

Dor Too many drinkers an' not enough doers.

Lane What about Barry? I thought you was in.

Dor He's staying after time.

Lane Why don't we?

Dor I don't fancy it.

Lane What we gonna do now, no fellahs, no money? I'm
not going home to *him.*

Dor I'm not going home to *him.* God I feel a bit wuzzy I
always do when I'm standing still. (*She puts her hand out and
leans on the wall.*)

Lane Eh. What was up with him tonight?

Dor Who?

Lane Teddy.

Dor Teddy behind the bar?

Lane Aye old long face. He never even let on.

Dor I know, I know. And we were close at one time you know. He give me and me cousin one once behind the pub.

Lane They're all the bastard same. God I wish you hadn't mentioned sex, I feel naughty now.

Dor I do. (*She has a coughing fit.*)

Lane Get it up.

Dor I wish somebody would.

Lane Ohhhhhhhhhh. (*Indicating the audience below.*) Well take your pick Lane love. Yoo hoo.

Dor (*choosing someone who resembles a celebrity*) What about Blake Carrington down there then.

Lane Come on.

They rush off as though to go down for him.

Scullery *crosses eating chips.*

Scullery Last orders is gone. Everybody's coming home a bit pissed. Piping hot these. (*He eats.*)

Scullery *exits.*

A young lad, **Curt,** *staggers on, chips in one hand. He grabs hold of a lamppost.*

Curt God I feel sick. God I'm frightened if I just turn, it'll be too much. God in here (*He touches his side.*) there's too much floating, too much. I'm not s'pose to drink with what I'm on, but I don't bother now. Enjoy what you can, while you can, if you can can. (*He sniffs.*) God it stinks this road. (*He sniffs.*) Staleness, rot, sick, sex, drink, blood. There's always been something wrong down here. It's where things slide to but don't drop off. Even darkness is different down here, it's all red and black like blood and ink, and you feel it in the throat. I'm ill. (*He starts coughing.*) Oh God I feel like I'm gonna throw. I don't wanna though. (*He wraps his arms tight round the post and holds on, clenching his teeth as though something's passing over him. He stops, looks out again.*) When you've been down for so long, under so much, you get like a pressed leaf, and stay that way forever. Brown, sick-white,

and flat. Aw. (*He lets go with one arm and lets himself swing.*)
Aw I'm sick of moaning. Be full of good cheer, if not then
bad beer. (*He taps his stomach.*) There you go.

*He throws his chips high in the air. They scatter everywhere. He
goes off.*

Blackout.

*Darkness except for a spotlight on an armchair centre stage. A
young **Soldier** is sitting in it, very drunk, staring out front. The
spotlight breaks out over the stage. He turns to see the door open.
An Alsatian dog crosses the room and goes out through the opposite
door.*

*Then **Helen** backs in with two plates. One has chips, pudding and
peas on it, one fish and chips. She shuts the door with her bum and
goes over to him.*

Helen Here they are love. I've put 'em on plates. Now
which is which? Hang on. You're pudding that means I'm
fish. Watch the gravy love it's dripping off one side.

*She gives it to him, lays it on his knees. She drags a pouffe in the
shape of a tortoise, over to the side of the armchair and sits by him.
Her suspenders show.*

They make a nice chip at the chinky don't they? Bit greasy.
Bet you miss this in the mess? Where's your camp anyway?
You never said. You don't say much do you? Take your
boots off if you like. Do you want the telly on? Well yes or
no? Oooooh, you're the real quiet type aren't you? Still
waters run deep or what? The Clint Eastwood type. Little
mini Clint. Eh, I like him though do you? I like loners.
That's why I sent Maureen to fetch you over tonight. That
uniform, dead romantic. It's ages since I've seen a soldier.
You just sort of stood out in the crowd. Would you kill
somebody if you had to? Say they provoked you. That's your
duty though in' it? This is what you get paid for. Licence to
kill. You must have a laugh though. All this one-armed
combat and what not. (*She sees something in her meal.*) What
the bloody hell's this? It's either mine or that bloody dog's.
I'll skin the beast. Kojak! Kojak! Come 'ere. Look at that.

She holds it up in front of the **Soldier**'s *face, a chip dangling on a long hair. He throws up into his meal. She gets up.*

Helen   Oh bloody hell. Oh heck.

She puts her chips down and goes off into the kitchen. The dog comes back on and starts eating her chips and fish. She comes back in with an old dirty towel.

Kojak you bastard! Get out of it! (*She shoos the dog off with the towel.*) You bloody dirty git.

The **Soldier** *looks up all lost and bleary.*

Helen   Not you cocker, him, that hound. (*She looks at him and the mess.*) Oh dear. Not to worry. (*She gets down and starts padding up the sick with the towel.*) I've got a flannel here cock. Let's just wipe your chops off.

She wipes his face like a baby. He fights a bit in his drunken stupor like a baby might. She pauses a moment in her wiping.

Aaaaw. (*She looks again, wipes on. She starts to loosen his tie.*) Look, it's all over your shirt and down your nice smart jacket. We can't have that can we now. Eh? No we cannot. (*She starts to unbutton his jacket. At first she's brisk and fast, then she slows down almost enjoying it. She pauses in thought. She gets up and goes over to the record player by the bed. It's on the floor, an old-fashioned mono-portable with a heavy arm. She picks a record up. The records are without sleeves just in a pile on the floor. Some are in an old wire record rack. She squats as she puts it on. As she gets it on and the automatic begins and it drops, she falls over.*) Oh bloody hell. (*She giggles. As she lies there she looks up at him.*)

The music starts (Barry Manilow or Frank Sinatra). She gets up and walks over to him. Now as she undresses him, the music has affected her, and she does it seductively. She gets the jacket and shirt off. She looks again at the **Soldier**. *She kisses him, very sloppy and round.*

Helen   Oh you are naughty. And so young as well. So young and full of it. I bet you've had loads of girls already 'ant you eh? (*She kisses him again.*) Why should you choose me eh? (*She gets his cheeks in her hands.*) Eh? Why? What have I got?

(*She puts her tongue in his ear.*) Oh you sexy bugger. Watch it. You really know what to do don't you? Not like most blokes. I bet you're the type that knows how to cherish a girl. (*She hugs him and puts her head on his chest.*) So firm. I imagine you've got the girls running round you like flies on muck. Why me? You could have your pick any time. (*She touches his mouth with her fingers.*) You could have your pick even of the famous stars. (*She kisses him again, she shifts position, she kneels in her plate of chips.*) Oh. (*She looks at him.*) Oh I am sorry I've kneeled in my chips. Forgive me. (*She stands up, picks them off her tights and drops them on the plate. She picks the plate up and goes over to put it on the sideboard. She sees the bed. She lies back on it in a sexy pose looking at him.*) Come on then. Oh you, you do play it cool. You know how to hold back and get a woman sexed. (*She looks at him.*) I know what we'll do. (*She rolls over and changes the record.*) I know. Just the job this one. Just the blinking job.

It starts blaring out. It's James Brown's Sex Machine. *She turns it up even louder. She rolls about a bit.*

Wheeeeeeeee. (*She goes over to him, arms outstretched.*) What you're gonna tak' me now. Just like that out the blue. Bloody soldiers. (*She grabs him up off the chair and holds him close.*) Oh. Oh. What you doing. Oh. Oh. Lover boy. Soldier of love.

They wobble back over to the bed.

Wow, you've been overseas haven't you? What a touch boy. Wowie.

She flops back on the bed, letting him go. He just falls on top of her, she wraps her legs round him quick.

Oh. Oh.

He slides off her into the record player and out on the floor. The music stops. She leans off the bed and over him.

Are you all right? (*She comes out of it a bit. She runs her finger over his face.*) You're like a little boy. (*She starts crying.*) I'm sorry. Oh dear.

She cries more. She gets up. Puts pillow under his head and blanket over him where he lies. Sits on the armchair drying her eyes.

I don't know what they think you are. They treat you like last week's muck. (*She looks like she's going to cry again. She closes her eyes and gently shakes her head.*) I feel right ashamed now. And so sad. (*She whispers it.*) So sad. (*She says it voiceless.*) So sad. (*She closes her eyes and puts her head back.*)

Blackout.

Back to the Road.

Blue light, spinning lights going round and round from a silver ball. Music playing: The Last Waltz (*Engelbert Humperdinck*). *It's like in a dance hall of the fifties.*

Jerry *comes on in a worn blue velvet jacket, shirt, tie. He is drunk and weepy-looking, eyes closed, dancing round and round with himself, across the stage.*

Scullery *appears, eating his last chip.*

He quickly screws up the chip papers in a ball and throws them at **Jerry**. *They bounce off his head. The music stops, the lights go down.*

Jerry *strolls off, lost.*

Blackout.

Scullery *exits.*

The lights come up. **Dor** *backs onstage looking for something. Can't see it. She leans on wall. From a window above, the sound of* **Mrs Bald** *singing* Somewhere Over The Rainbow.

Bald (*off*) Shut it!

Silence.

Barry *enters, drunk. He has a pool cue. He takes a few pots.*

Barry (*to the audience*) Pool King me.

Dor Barry.

Barry (*looks round*) How you doing? Do you fancy a bit?

Dor Not at the moment.

Barry Got a light?

Dor *strikes a match for him.*

Above, **Bald**'s *face is squashed against the glass.*

Bald Put that light out!

They both look up.

He's gone.

Barry What's up anyroad?

Dor I've lost me bastard keys. I'm locked out.

Barry *laughs.*

Dor Help me find 'em.

Barry No way. (*He pulls a bottle of beer out of each pocket.*) Have you got an opener?

Dor There's one on me key-ring.

Barry You look there! I'll look here!

As they search, they speak to the audience.

Dor You seen a key?

Barry Seen a key love?

Barry *goes down on all fours searching; can't be seen.*

Bald *opens the window.*

Bald Hey what you looking for?

Dor A key.

Bald Well fuck off then!

Dor Shove it you miserable old crow.

Bald You what! What did you say!!

Barry (*suddenly standing*) She said shut your stink hole fat face!

Bald (*meekly*) Oh I see I just wondered. 'Bye.

He goes back in.

Barry (*holding the bottles out*) Where's this opener? (*Up to the window*.) Oy you! Oy Rambo! Have you got opener!

The window opens and **Bald** *appears.*

Bald (*a tirade*) What do you think this is eh! Keeping decent ones awake like this. My wife's awake here.

Mrs Bald I'm not.

Bald You are! It's bloody disgusting. Hey an' I know your husband.

Dor So do I.

Bald Shouting up the road. Drunks. Hooligans . . . (*Etc. etc.*)

Barry (*shouting over the noise*) Hey. Hey. I'll tell you what. Deal. Opener for a bottle.

Bald *suddenly stops shouting. He goes in.*

An opener comes out, hits the ground.

Barry *picks it up. He motions to* **Dor**. *They go.* **Bald** *appears at the window with his special tankard.*

Bald Hey hey what about deal!?

They can be heard laughing offstage.

Bald *looks out, goes in.*

Mrs Bald (*off*) Sucker.

Bald (*off*) Shut it.

Mrs Bald (*off*) He he he.

Blackout.

The lights come up on a woman waiting, smoking. She is in her mid-thirties, sitting on a hard kitchen chair. She has a scruffy dressing-gown on, a bit of sad nightie showing.

Valerie I'm fed up of sitting here waiting for him, he'll be another hundred years at his rate. What a life, get up, feed every baby in the house. Do everything else I can, without cash. While he drinks, drinks it, drinks it, and shoves

nothing my way except his fat hard hands in bed at night.
Rough dog he is. Big rough heavy dog. Dog with sick in its
fur. He has me pulling my hair out. Look at my hair, it's so
dry. So sadly dried. I'd cry but I don't think tears would
come. And there's nothing worse than an empty cry. It's like
choking. Why do we do it? Why do I stay? Why the why
why? You can cover yourself in questions and you're none
the wiser 'cause you're too tired to answer. Always scrimping
and scraping. He just takes the Giro and does what he wants
with it. Leaves a few pounds on the table corner sometimes,
sometimes. But you never know when and if you ask him he
chops you one. That's why I have to borrow, borrow off
everyone. I am like a bony rat going here, going there,
trying to sniffle something out. They help me, though I'll
bet you they hate me really. Despise me really. Because I'm
always there an' keep asking, asking and they can't say no.
They just open their purses, and I says, thank you, thank
you a thousand times till we all feel sick. God I can't wait till
the kids are older then I can send them. He'll come in soon.
Pissed drunk through. Telling me I should do more about
the place. Eating whatever's in the house. Pissing and
missing the bog. Squeezing the kids too hard. Shouting then
sulking. Then sleeping all deep and smelly, wrapped over
and over in the blankets. Drink's a bastard. Drink's a swilly
brown bastard. A smelling stench sea. And he's the captain
with his bristles wet through. Swallowing and throwing,
swallowing and throwing white brown water all over me. Oh
what am I saying, it's a nightmare all this. I blame him then
I don't blame him. It's not his fault there's no work. He's
such a big man, he's nowhere to put himself. He looks so
awkward and sad at the sink, the vacuum's like a toy in his
hand. When he's in all day he fills up the room. Like a big
wounded animal, moving about, trying to find his slippers,
clumsy with the small things of the house, bewildered. I see
this. I see the poor beast in the wrong world. I see his eyes
sad and low. I see him as the days go on, old damp sacks
one on top of another. I see him, the waste. The human
waste of the land. But I can't forgive him. I can't forgive the
cruel of the big fucking heap. The big fucking clumsy heap.
(*She startles herself with what she's saying, nearly cries.*) He's so
big and hunched and ugly. (*Holding back.*) Oh my man. (*She*

chokes.) I hate him now, and I didn't used to. I hate him now, and I don't want to. (*She cries.*) Can we not have before again, can we not? (*She cries.*) Can we not have before again? (*She looks out manic and abrupt.*) Can we not?

Blackout.

The sound of **Chantal**'s *song. The lights come up as she appears, still singing to herself, toying with a cigarette. (This next bit should be improvised around who she sees etc., etc.) She flirts with men in the audience.*

Chantal (*to a man*) Have you got a light? (*She moves on to another, sings a bit.*) Have you got one Smiley? (*She moves on.*) Have you got a light?

She likes this one. She goes over to him, plays with his tie, leads him off by it to the nearest exit. As they go . . .

Bald *appears.*

Bald (*from the window above*) CHANTAL! CHANTAL!

Chantal What!

Bald Get in. Your mother's worried.

Mrs Bald (*off*) I'm not.

Bald You are!

Chantal *carries on out with the man.*

Bald *disappears.*

Blackout.

Back to the Road.

Scullery *comes on pissed and staggering.*

Scullery Blowpipe! Blowpipe! Blowpipe! Blowpipe!

Blowpipe *appears.*

Scullery Where you bin? (*He smacks him on top of his cap.*)

Blowpipe Rustling. (*He pulls out a full bottle of unopened rum.*)

Scullery (*takes it*) Ah my saviour. (*He kisses him. He kisses the bottle. He holds it out to the audience at arm's length.*)

He links arms with **Blowpipe** *and they set off.*

As they go off they pass a drunk woman, **Marion,** coming on with **Brian.**

Marion Scullduggery!

Scullery Marion!

Brian *pulls at her.*

Scullery Where you goin'?

Marion Being brushed off my feet.

They go off on the other side from **Scullery** *and* **Blowpipe.**

The lights come up on a living-room.

Marion *and* **Brian** *come in really pissed. She flops on the couch. He stands over her, pulls his zip down.*

Marion (*pushing him away*) No I want a butty first.

Brian (*indicating the kitchen*) Well there's some bloody luncheon meat in there. Get one.

Marion Bloody hell. Bloody hell eh, can't even mak' us summat eat now.

Brian Ahrrgh.

She stumbles into the kitchen.

He goes over to sideboard and gets a bottle of sherry out. She screams. He drunkenly stumbles round.

She comes in, blood dripping all over her thumb.

Marion I cut me bleeding thumb.

He stumbles over to her, gets hold of her all lovey, puckering his lips in sympathy.

Get off. (*She goes to the couch, to her handbag, opens it, drops it.*) Sodding hell. (*She gets a tissue out, holds it on.*)

He comes over and sits next to her on the couch, puts his arm round her. They let their heads drop together and talk drunkenly, like two babies.

Brian How my likkle luv?

Marion Thumb.

Brian Naughty thumb.

Marion It sore.

Brian Aawwwwwwwwww. Cum here.

Holds her, kisses her, catches her thumb.

Marion Owwwww. Get off!

She pushes him off. He lies back on the couch. She does also.

Give us a swig.

He gives her the bottle, stands up, burps, takes it back.

Eh eh, I've not finished yet. (*She grabs at it.*)

Brian You don't think you're having all me drink and not giving us a shag do you?

Marion (*snatches the drink off him*) I don't tease a man me. No way. I wouldn't give you a jack on then leave you. Come on Brian you know me better than that. (*She swigs it.*) Get us a glass anyroad. Where's your manners.

She rubs herself up against him. He's so pissed he nearly falls over.

Brian (*laughing*) Ha ha. Aye.

He goes in the kitchen.

She has another swig, pulls her bra straight.

He comes back with a big pint glass, gives it to her.

She doesn't seem to bother, just pours drink in it. Both are still standing and tottering.

Marion Where's your daughter?

He motions upstairs, puts his head on his hands; he means sleeping.
Marion *drinks. She falls back on the couch.*

Put a record on.

He walks stiff-legged over to the record player and puts Country and Western on very loud.

(*Approves.*) Hey hey. (*She lifts the glass.*)

He comes back over to her, gets on the couch, starts holding her, kissing the side of her cheek big and round. She turns round, grabs his head, starts snogging him hard.

The door opens and **Linda** *comes in, about twelve-years-old, long hair, night-gown.* **Marion** *stops.*

They look at **Linda***. She looks at them.*

Linda I can't sleep for allt' noise, Dad.

Marion Is this her Brian? Well, she's bloody gorgeous, bloody gorgeous, her.

Brian Aye she's a good 'un.

Marion Come here, love.

The girl reluctantly comes over to the back of the settee. **Marion** *kneels up on the couch, gets the girl's head and kisses her. The girl is trying to pull back.*

Lovely.

Blood goes on the girl's face from **Marion***'s thumb. The girl touches it, looks at her Father.*

Marion What's up cock? Oh that's mine, off here. (*She shows her thumb.*) The pig did it, him. (*She slaps him, playful.*) Not making me nowt to eat. Come and sit down here love. Me neck's going. (*She grabs her hand and drags her round and between them both.*) Hold on. (*She goes in her bag and pulls out a tissue, spits on it and starts wiping the girl's face.*) There you are cock. Eh don't be scared. Eh. (*She puts her arm round her.*) Brian, turn that bleeding music down or off or summat, for me an' her. We don't like it loud do we. (*She is taking the girl's hair back behind her ear.*) Eh not.

The girl looks miserable. **Brian** *goes and turns the music down. He picks up the bottle, swigs from it.*

Brian (*to* **Marion**) Come on upstairs.

Marion Hold your horses. We're talking here. What do you want to be when you grow up luv?

The girl shrugs.

Well whatever it is luv, stick at it and you'll get there.

Brian *grabs* **Marion**'s *shoulder.*

Brian Come on now.

She knocks his hand off.

Marion Who's your favourite pin-up star, luv? Do you like them Agadoo?

He pokes her.

Eh! (*To the girl.*) Men.

The girl looks upset. He pokes her again.

Brian Come on.

Marion Hang on.

He pokes her.

No.

She looks to the girl. She's crying. **Marion** *puts her arm round her. The girl slips free.*

Aw love, Aw. Cheer up cock. (*She turns to* **Brian**, *angry with him.*) Here you. Put fucking Agadoo on for her. (*She shoves him towards the record player.*)

He stops half-way.

Brian I'm going.

He sets off for the door. He goes out, leaving door open, then goes out the front door.

Marion Hey hang on. (*To the girl.*) Miserable swine he is. Hey come back.

She gets up and goes out the door. The front door slams, off.

The girl picks up the bottle off the floor and collects the tissues. She straightens the couch up, turns to exit. On her way, she stops, turns back.

Linda (*to the audience, mocking*) POOR LITTLE ME!

She exits.

A rattling is heard getting louder and louder. Suddenly **Scullery** *enters pushing a shopping trolley at mad speed across the stage.*

Scullery Ayeeeeeeeeeeeeeeeeeeeeeee! (*He turns it and comes back to centre stage.*) Ayeeeeeeeeeeeeeeeeeeeeeee!

As this happens, **Brian** *comes on pursued by* **Marion**.

Marion Come here you!

Brian Aw piss off!

Marion What's the fucking big idea?!

Brian Aw fuck off, woman!

Marion I'll fuck nowhere. You stand still!

Scullery *is enjoying this. He sits in the trolley to watch.*

Brian Go with your little friend.

Marion Oh you nasty-minded bugger!

She grabs him, makes him stop. They end up on each side of the trolley. **Scullery** *smack in the middle.*

You're a selfish bastard you, Brian. Me myself an' I! Me myself an' I!

Brian Aw fuck off.

Marion You know what your pissing problem is don't you eh?

Brian What?

Marion You don't know how to treat a woman.

Brian You know what your pissin' problem is don't you?

Marion What!

Brian You're not woman, you're tart.

She loses her temper more, goes for him, but he spins the trolley round between them. Now they're on opposite sides to before.

Marion FART!

Brian TART!

Madder still at this, she gives chase again. Again he spins round putting the trolley between them.

Marion (*can't get at him*) Arrrghgh!

Brink *and* **Eddie** *appear in the gallery.*

Brink Where they gone?

Eddie Don't know, they said wait here a minute.

Brink (*seeing the row*) Look at that!

Eddie come on!

They set off down.

Onstage **Brian** *leaves.*

Marion Eh come back you! I've not finished wi' you!

She goes off after him. They run through the theatre.

Brian Away woman!

Marion No way!

Brian Piss off out of it!

Marion No way! No way! You lousy dick! Stop still! STOP STILL! STOP!

Brian Are you fucking mental altogether?

Marion You will be if I fuckin' clouts ya!

Brian Silly cow!

Marion What was that? What was fucking that! HOLD STILL YOU, YOU BASTARD!

They exit.

Carol *and* **Louise** *enter onstage. They hear the shouting.*

Carol What's goin' on?

Louise Oh bloody hell fire.

Carol What's goin' on Scull?

Scullery Fight night. (*His hands to his mouth.*) Dong dong seconds away round two.

Brian *and* **Marion** *appear on the circle.*

Marion I'll kill you, Brian. I'll kill! I'm not joking.

Brink *and* **Eddie** *appear in the circle.*

Brink Go on, love!

Eddie Give him one!

Marion Piss OFF! OR YOU'LL PISSIN' GET IT!

Brink Promises.

She swings for him with her handbag. **Eddie** *goes up behind her, slaps her backside. She hits him with her bag.*

Marion Prick!

From below.

Carol (*shouting up*) Eh!

Louise Eh!

Carol Come down lads!

Louise Come down.

Scullery Stay up!

Louise *hits him.*

Carol You're like bloody big kids, leave her!

Marion *comes forward and leans over to shout down.*

Marion Oh listen little madam there. I can fight me own fucking battles, thank you!

Brink *and* **Eddie** *crack up laughing at this.*

Carol You slag!

Louise You bloody fat slag!

Marion Aw fuck you.

Carol Watch it woman!

Louise Old slut!

Marion (*spits*) Piss off, young bitches.

Brian What a state to be in.

Marion You what! This is your cunting fault all this! Get here now!

Eddie Eh you're lovely when your angry!

Marion Fuck off shrimp!

Brink What a lady.

Marion Don't push it, boy!

Brink I wun't push nowt in you, lovey.

Marion You young cunt. (*She goes for him.*)

Scullery Get in there!

Louise Ignore her an' come down!

Carol Come on!

Louise Come on!

Carol Leave the old bag!

Brian *leaves*.

Scullery There he goes love!

Marion (*turning round*) Eh eh come back, Brian. Come back!

She goes after him.

The lads come down onstage.

Carol Where've you two been. I thought you were waiting for us.

Brink Well, we're here now.

Scullery *is still in the shopping trolley.*

Scullery Hey I'm on special offer; don't miss your bargain, girls.

Carol *and* **Louise** *look at each other, smile, grab the trolley and shove him off.*

Scullery (*as he goes*) OOOhhhhhhhhhhhhhhhhhhhhh.

Marion *and* **Brian** *appear at the very top gallery in spotlights.*

Marion You've shown me up tonight 'an't you eh! You fat arsed twat.

Brian Get home cow!

Marion Never, you cunt!

Brian Get home!

Marion BRIAN! BRIAN! THE BASTARD BLEEDING FUCK!

Blackout.

Brink *and* **Eddie** *and* **Carol** *and* **Louise** *go towards* **Brink**'s *place.*

The lights come up on **Brink**'s *place. A long settee, two chairs, a massive stereo speaker, like bands have, in the corner; by it, a flat record deck; on the wall, hung by a gold nail, is a single record.*

Eddie *enters first; he has five bottles of wine in his arms. He unloads them all on the end of the long settee.* **Brink** *enters. Then* **Carol** *and* **Louise** *come in together, giggling.*

Eddie Take a seat girls, I'll get some glasses.

Carol Why, can you not see?

The girls both giggle.

Eddie Eh?

They giggle again.

Eddie *shrugs, smiles and goes in the kitchen.*

Brink Come on have a seat. (*To the audience, if promenade.*)
You too.

Brink *goes off into the kitchen.*

*The girls walk around the settee together to front centre stage. They
stand looking around. They look at each other and start giggling
again.*

Eddie (*off, from the kitchen*) Just tryin' to find a corkscrew!

Carol That's nice.

They both laugh. **Carol** *starts throwing things off the couch onto
one of the chairs, one at a time.*

Lovely place you got here. (*She pulls a face at* **Louise**.)

Eddie Do you think so?

Carol Oh definitely. I thought I was int' Ritz for a minute.

*They both sit down really close to each other up one end of the
settee.*

Eddie *comes in with glasses and a corkscrew. He puts them down.*

Eddie Here we are.

Carol (*looking behind*) Where's whatsisname then?

Eddie Oh he's just coming.

The sound of a toilet flush rattling loud, off. **Carol** *and* **Louise**
burst out really laughing. **Eddie** *just hands out the glasses.*

Brink *enters. He goes and sits on an armchair.*

Carol Hiyah.

Brink *smiles.* **Louise** *titters.* **Eddie** *is getting the corkscrew in a
bottle. He opens two bottles, one red one white.*

Is he t'waiter then?

Brink No, he's just better at it than me.

Carol What a confession.

Louise *laughs.* **Carol** *stays straight-faced.*

Brink What? Oh yeah. Ha.

Both girls crack up laughing.

Eddie Here we go. (*He gets up, starts pouring the wine, to* **Carol** *first.*)

Carol Hang on, is that white?

Eddie Yeah.

Carol Aw, I wanted red.

Eddie Oh. (*He goes back and gets the red.*)

Carol Er no, go on. I'll have white.

Eddie *comes towards her with bottle.*

Oh I don't know though, red's good in' it?

Eddie (*laughing*) I'll pour it over your head in a minute.

Carol Oh God Louise, in' he masterful? (*Holds out her glass.*) Go on then pour.

He does. He passes on to **Louise**.

Er waiter, what's your name again?

Eddie Eddie.

Carol Eh, Eddie you know what they say, don't you?

Eddie What?

Carol White and they're up all night. (*She drinks.*) Red, . they're straight to bed.

Louise *splutters.*

Eddie Oh aye, an' who told you that?

Carol (*sips*) She did.

Louise I never!

Carol Did you not? Well I thought you did. Never mind. Carry on. Carry on.

He pours some for **Brink** *and himself. They all drink.*

Brink So what do you do?

Carol What do you fancy?

Louise *tuts.*

Eddie What do you mean?

Carol (*pretending to change the subject*) Er nice wine, in' it?

Louise No.

They both laugh.

Eddie (*tries again*) So what do you do?

Brink (*quickly*) To live.

Carol Well I breathe, I can't speak for her like.

Louise *splutters.*

Eddie I don't know, you're quick you two aren't you?

Carol No, you two are slow.

Louise *spills her drink on herself, drops the glass. It breaks.*

Louise Oh look!

Eddie I'll get you a cloth.

Eddie *goes off into the kitchen.* **Brink** *gets up and goes too.*

Carol (*shouts*) God, how big is this cloth. Take two corners each then just walk in with it!

Louise Oh Carol. Do you not like 'em?

Carol They're okay. But they just think they're great.

Louise Eh? They're a bit of all right though aren't they?

Carol Did you not see 'em at the bar posing off?

Louise I know, but you fancied 'em when you saw 'em.

Carol Maybe I did. Maybe I did. And the way they chatted us up.

Louise I know, but it were good though weren't it? Very different.

Carol You could say that. They just think too much of themselves for my liking.

Louise I think they're all right.

Carol Well, no ways are they gettin' the better of me.

Eddie *comes back in. He goes to* **Louise** *and gives her a cloth. He gets down and starts picking up bits of glass.*

Carol (*looking round*) Where's he gone again? Is there summat wrong with his bowels or what?

Eddie (*laughs*) He's just looking for another glass for Louise.

Louise *gives him back the cloth, he starts mopping up the couch arm and floor with it.*

Brink *appears in the doorway.*

Brink There's not another one. You can have mine.

Louise No, it's all right.

Eddie (*passing it to her*) You're all right, here you are.

Louise Oh I don't want to take your glass. What'll you have?

Carol *grabs it out of* **Eddie**'s *hand.*

Carol Here get it. Sap. (*She gets the bottle and pours more wine.*) Here and top it up.

Louise Carol!

Brink *has a mug with him.* **Eddie** *sits on the couch with the girls.* **Brink** *sits on the arm of the armchair.* **Carol** *looks at* **Eddie**, *then looks at* **Brink**.

Carol Eh what's this? Manoeuvres. We're being surrounded, Louise cock.

Brink (*to* **Louise**) Is she always like this?

Louise Yes.

Carol Hang on a minute. Like what?

Brink Like . . .

Carol What!

Brink Aggressive.

Carol In what way? What's that s'pose to mean?

Brink I don't know.

Eddie He's sorry he spoke.

Carol Sorry he spoke. I should think so. I'm not aggressive. (*She grabs* **Louise**, *mock-nuts her*.) Am I not, Louise love?

Louise (*laughs*) I'm saying nowt.

Carol Anyway, what does mean, aggressive? I'm just having a bit of fun. If you can't take that there's summat wrong with you.

Brink We can take it.

Carol I s'pose you're not used to this, you're used to women just fallin' all over you, aren't you?

Brink Not really, no.

Carol Just fallin' all under you then.

Brink *smiles*.

Carol Dick.

Brink She's mad.

Eddie She's not.

Carol I am.

Louise She is.

They all laugh. Pause.

Eddie (*holding up a bottle high*) Anybody want some more?

Carol (*holding up her glass high*) Not yet.

Pause.

How long you lived here?

Brink *shrugs*.

Carol Well it's certainly a . . . certainly a . . . what's that word I'm looking for?

Eddie Tip?

Carol No, slag heap.

Louise *laughs*.

Carol That's it.

Eddie Eh, well feel free, girls, to put it in order.

Carol You must be a joke.

Louise You must be joking. You want to see the state of her room at home.

Carol Louise shut up givin' away my personals. You'll be telling 'em what colour knickers I've got on next. (*She looks at them.*) Go on, say it. 'If you had any on' or 'See-through'.

Brink I'm saying nothing.

Carol Oh what gentlemen, or are you just pouffs?

Louise Carol, you're terrible.

Carol Eh, eh Louise don't desert the ranks now. Especially when they're just coming on so strong, eh lads?

They just smile.

So now we're round to it. When are you going to move in then, lads? When should we expect the first move?

Brink *leans right over and starts kissing her.*

Carol Get off.

He stops and stands.

Get off.

Brink *goes back to the chair, unaffected.*

Brink (*hands up*) I'm off.

She's a bit stunned.

Carol (*to compose herself*) I thought I could smell summat.

No one laughs. **Brink** *sits away in the chair.* **Eddie** *drinks.*

Louise It's nice this place really.

Eddie Really?

Louise (*laughs*) I mean underneath it all. If it was tidied up.

Eddie I s'pose it's not bad it's . . .

Carol (*to* **Brink**) So are you not speaking now? (*Not giving him time to answer; to* **Eddie**.) Is he sulking now?

Brink No. Not at all. Nothing like that.

Carol (*looking at them both one to another*) I don't know where I am with you two.

Eddie What do you mean?

Louise (*excited*) You're right different.

Eddie Than what?

Carol (*quick*) Watch it Louise they'll get all big-headed. Well bigger-headed. (*She scrutinizes them both.*) What is it with you two?

Brink *reaches out and takes* **Louise**'s *hand. He leads her over towards him, stands and kisses her.*

Carol (*looks. She gets up, goes into the kitchen. Off.*) Is it through here?

Eddie What?

No reply. **Eddie** *realizes she means the toilet.*

Oh yeah yeah. Straight through.

Louise *separates from* **Brink** *though still in his arms.*

Brink What is it?

Louise Carol.

Brink *looks at her.*

She's gone off 'cause she likes you really.

Brink (*recognizing something in her*) And what about you, who do you like?

She looks down, a bit embarrassed.

You like Eddie really, don't you?

She looks a bit more embarrassed.

It's all right. Eddie.

Eddie *stands up and takes* **Louise** *back with him onto his knee in one single movement.*

Brink *goes off through to the kitchen.*

Eddie *kisses* **Louise** *very gently, and again. She puts her hand in his hair. From the kitchen is heard:*

Carol (*off*) What's this? Hey. You soon change your tune.

Then movement as he kisses her. Then they enter. He turns the light off.

The stage is in darkness. Black. Sounds of kissing and movement. Shuffling. **Carol** *says 'No'. Movement.* **Carol** *says 'Get off'. Shuffling.* **Carol** *turns the light on.*

That's enough of that.

Carol *is standing at the light switch.* **Louise** *has moved away from* **Eddie.**

Carol What do you think we are?

Brink *shrugs.*

Carol What do you think we are, slags?

Eddie Nooo.

Brink Why did you come back?

Carol Just for something to do.

Brink What about all the lead ons, lead ins?

Louise Don't he talk funny. You were like that in the pub. Lead on, lead ins.

Eddie (*changing the subject*) Anyway.

Louise (*turning on him realizing she should be mad*) Anyway what?

Eddie Eh eh. Don't be bad-tempered. Anyway, more drinks? (*He lifts the bottle.*)

Carol You can't get us drunk then start again you know.

Brink Forget it.

Carol Listen him now. Typical. They're all the same. Can't get their end away they don't wanna know. Do get their end away they don't wanna know.

Eddie Oh come on.

Carol No. I want somethin' else to happen for a change. It's the same every time. Every time some smart-arse spends time and money on you with one thing only in mind. Then upsets you. It's boring and upsetting. I'm sick of it. You think you're just wanted for use. You two seemed a bit interesting, a bit unusual like. I thought I might find something else here. But not so. You're always wrong, aren't you? Nowt's never the way you wanted. You always have to make do. Every single thing's a disappointment.

Louise Carol.

Carol *stops.*

Carol Come on then Louise. (*She gets her bag.*)

Louise *gets hers, they start leaving.*

Eddie Come on, have another.

They go for the door. **Brink** *suddenly jumps up really quick, the fastest thing he's done all night, and stands in front of the door.*

Brink Stay and I promise you something different. Let's see how much difference you can take.

Carol *stops in her tracks. So does* **Louise.**

You want something different. Stay, I mean it. (*He guides them back to the settee.*) You know what we do for it. To really get a change. We have a something that we always do when outside gets to you. Eddie, shall we show them?

Eddie *looks.*

Come on let's show them. Let's have it out of them.

The girls sit, mystified.

Do you like good music?

Carol Yeah. Like what?

Brink Like soul. Real down there soul.

Carol Don't know what you mean.

While he's talking, **Eddie** *is pouring wine in the glasses.*

Brink What about you, Louise?

Louise Well I like 'Hot Chocolate'.

Brink *shakes his head.* **Eddie** *is passing around glasses.*

Eddie Drink.

They hesitate.

Brink Drink. Don't worry, go on.

Eddie Go.

They do.

Fast though. Fast!

They do.

Brink Good.

Eddie *is quickly filling up the glasses again.*

Carol Eh, hang on.

Brink *grabs one up and drinks it.*

Eddie Do. Another?

Brink Another.

Carol What you doing?

The lads are laughing. **Eddie** *fills up again.*

Brink It's all part of it, you'll see after.

Eddie (*lifts his glass*) Brink old drink.

They cheer and clink glasses, then drink. **Louise** *laughs.* **Carol**
does a bit.

Brink Come on Eddie, steady.

They lift the glasses and down them. **Eddie** *lets himself fall back.*
Carol *suddenly laughs too.*

Come on in. Join us.

He touches her chin. She knocks his hand away.

Carol All right, set 'em up.

Louise Carol.

Carol Oh what the hell.

Eddie *has already set them up. They get a glass each.*

Brink Down.

He opens his mouth wide first. **Eddie** *too. They pour it down in
one.* **Carol** *and* **Louise** *laugh and giggle, try it but can't get it
down so fast, but manage to shift it.* **Eddie** *is opening another two
bottles.*

Carol What about some music then?

Brink Some will be coming soon and . . .

Carol And what?

Brink Wait for it, love.

Louise Oooooh.

They drink again.

Carol Come on put summat on now, what you got? Let's
see.

Eddie *drinking, points to the single on the wall.*

Carol Eh just that one!

Eddie Aye that's it.

Brink One more drink, then it's on.

Eddie Up up.

The glasses are raised.

Carol This is mad.

Louise (*laughing*) It is in' it?

They drink them down.

Carol Music!

Brink Put it on.

Louise Put it on.

Eddie *gets up and puts the record on the deck.*

Carol Bloody hell I hope I like it.

Brink *slowly puts a finger to his mouth to quiet her. Silence. In the silence begins the slow crackling you always get with old records. The record is* Try a Little Tenderness *by Otis Redding. The volume is up very loud. The record ends.* **Eddie** *takes off from there.*

Eddie Bzzzzzzzzzzzzzzzzzzzzz. Raaaaaaaaaaaaaaaaaa. Blast off! Wyatt Earp, Wild Bill Hickock, Jesse James, Buffalo Bill, Billy the Kid, Maverick, Jim Bowie, Geronimo, Butch Cassidy, Davy Crockett, Doc Holiday, Eddie, Eddie, Eddie the hero. This is it, you let owt out, show what's below, let go, throw, glow, burn your Giro. I got me suit I got me image, suit, image. (*He sings.*) 'Who could ask for anything more?' Me! England's in pieces. England's an old twat in the sea. England's cruel. My town's scuffed out. My people's pale. Pale face. (*He pulls a pretend gun.*) Bang Bang Bang. It's a shoot-out with the sheriff. EDDIE, EDDIE, EDDIE, the hero. Don't weaken, or you're Dole and Done, Dole and Done, never weaken, show yoursel' sharp, so sharp you cut. Head up. Eyes hard. Walk like Robert Mitchum. (*He draws and shoots.*) Bang, Bang, Bang, Bang, Bang, Bang, Bang. I'm going to lie out now and burn for all I'm worth. (*He stops, lies down.*)

Silence. The girls' faces are wide open, stunned and drunk.

Brink That's what you do, you drink, you listen to Otis, you get to the bottom of things and let rip.

Louise (*in wonder*) What for?

Brink To stop going mad.

Louise Oh.

Carol *is quiet, swigging from the bottle. Hiccups.*

Louise (*drunk*) Give us a swig on that.

Carol Does he have to shout?

Brink I'm full of something nasty tonight. A smelly memory I can't wipe off. I'm s'pose to be the strong silent type me but I'm not. It's just a casing, in casing I get it again. Once I fucked an older woman, hated and fucked her hard on the kitchen floor, knees hitting the fridge, dog bowl in her hair, handfuls of old white skin in my mit. After she'd gone I sat on the lino and cried. My first skrike since 'No mummy left'. I always keep tight in front of people me, I don't want them in, they stink. HANDS OFF FOREVER! I want to be free. I want to be a cowboy, those dream fellows who died for us. Guns and smoke, one more dead a mouthful of saloon dust. I want cowboy but I'm just cattle, herded, helpless, waiting, aching to be killed, at the mercy of my CUNT-TRAY. Oh God on I crow. Down I go. I lie to myself. I lie to the Pope. I lie on the rug. I lie with my bedtime cheese. I must stop now because I'm crying real tears, but inside. A man cry. I cry through the dole, hole, times in which we live. Them slag's hands I still feel and I don't know why.

Carol *stands.*

Carol Can I say anything? Can I? I'll say this then. BIG BUST. BIG BUST ON ME BODY. BIG BRA BURSTING BUST. MEN LOOK. How's that? CRACK CRACK CRACK the whip on 'em. Crackoh crack, cut men for their sins. POVERTY. Poverty wants me. He's in my hair and clothes. He comes dust on me knickers. I can't scrape him off. Everythin's soiled you know, our house, me mum, the bath. I'm sick. Nowt's nice around me. Nowt's nice. NOWT'S NICE. Where's finery? Fucked off! Where's soft? Gone hard! I want a walk on the mild side. I want to be clean.

Cleaned. Spray me wi' somethin' sweet, spray me away. (*Stated*.) Carol has nowt.

Carol *sits, falls over to one side, curls up on the couch.*

Louise It's all gambling this, in't it? Gambling with gabble to see what come out. That record it's so about pure things it make you want to cry. Why's the world so tough? It's like walking through meat in high heels. Nothing's shared out right, money or love. I'm a quiet person me. People think I'm deaf and dumb. I want to say things but it hard. I have big wishes, you know? I want my life to be all shine'id up. It's so dull. Everything's so dulled. When that man sings on that record there, you put the flags up. Because he reminds you of them feelings you keep forgetting. The important ones. Once you wrap 'em up and put 'em away, there's nothing left but profit and loss and who shot who? But it's so hard, life. So hard. Nothing's interesting. Everything's been made ordinary in our eyes. I want magic and miracles. I want a Jesus to come and change things again and show the invisible. And not let us keep forgetting, forge-netting everything, kickin' everyone. I want the surface up and off and all the gold and jewels and light out on the pavements. Anyway I never spoke such speech in my life and I'm glad I have. If I keep shouting somehow a somehow I might escape.

Eddie Somehow a somehow, might escape.

Pause.

Somehow a somehow, might escape.

Brink Somehow a somehow, might escape.

Eddie
Brink   } (*together*) Somehow a somehow, might escape.

Louise Somehow a somehow, might escape.

Eddie
Brink   } (*together*) Somehow a somehow, might escape.
Louise

Carol (*coming up*) Somehow.

Eddie
Carol   } (*together*) Somehow a somehow a somehow,
Brink   might escape.
Louise

They all move in together.

All Somehow a somehow a somehow – (*Snatched.*) – might escape!

All pressed together, arms and legs round each other.

Somehow a somehow a somehow – might escape!

Out to the audience. A chant now.

Somehow a somehow a somehow – might escape!
Somehow a somehow a somehow – might escape!
Somehow a somehow a somehow – might escape!

Faster.

Somehow a somehow a somehow – might escape!
Somehow a somehow a somehow – might escape!
Somehow a somehow a somehow – might escape!

Very fast and loud.

SOMEHOW A SOMEHOW A SOMEHOW – MIGHT
ESCAPE!
SOMEHOW A SOMEHOW A SOMEHOW – MIGHT
ESCAPE!
SOMEHOW A SOMEHOW A SOMEHOW – MIGHT
ESCAPE!

Loud and massive.

SOMEHOOOOOOOOOO –

Blackout.

– OOOOOOOOOOOOOOOW.

Silence.

The lights come up on the Road.

Scullery *is just sliding his back down the wall to sit.*

Scullery Well it coming up to morning nar. I'll ha' a last fag and a last sup then I'll go whome. (*He takes a fag packet out, opens it, it's empty. He takes a bottle out of his pocket, puts it to his mouth, nothing in it. He turns it upside down, empty. He lets his head flop forward.*)

The lights dim on him. The sound of shoes dropping in the dark. The lights come up on **Helen** *in her room. She is sitting taking her shoes off. She strolls over to the bed, sits on it, lies down. The lights dim. The sound of dreamy humming. The lights come up on* **Jerry** *darning his sock, humming a good old tune. The lights dim. The sound of a bottle rolling. The lights come up on the four in* **Brink's** *room.* **Brink** *is asleep on the couch,* **Carol** *is asleep on the floor, her hand gently rolling a bottle.* **Eddie** *and* **Louise** *are standing in the centre of the room locked in an embrace, slowly swaying to some imagined music. The lights dim, then come up on* **Scullery,** *who is preparing to sleep where he is.*

Scullery If you're ever in the area call again. (*He lies down.*) Call again.

Blackout.

Production Notes

A shorter version of the play may be preferred and the following notes give an alternative.

Follow Act One as shown to the end of the **Eddie** and **Dad** scene (page 18).

Cut to **Molly** scene (page 21).

Return to **Scullery, Eddie, Brink, Lane, Dor** and **Skin-Lad** (page 18).

Cut the scene with the **Professor, Lane, Chantal** and **Scullery** (page 22 to 25).

Continue with **Skin-Lad**'s speech (page 25).

Continue following scene with **Scullery** in the derelict house, but cut the section with **Brenda** and **Scullery** (page 27 and 28).

Continue following scene – **Jerry**'s speech (page 30).

Continue following scene – **Scullery, Blowpipe** and **Molly** (page 31) but cut section with **Clare** (page 32).

Continue following scene with **Joey** and **Clare** and on to end of Act One.

In Act Two, if the theatre is not large enough to take the run around of the long argument (page 65 to 69), this shorter version can be used:

Begin scene as shown (page 65) and continue up to –

Marion (*can't get at him*) Arrrghrgh! (page 66)

Substitute next section of scene (page 66 to 68) with the following:

Brink, Eddie, Carol *and* **Louise** *enter. They see the row and watch.*

Marion I'll kill you Brian! I'll kill! I'm not joking!

Brian *laughs*.

Brink Go on love!

Marion Piss OFF! OR YOU'LL PISSIN' GET IT!!

Brink Promises.

She hits at **Brink** *with her handbag. They are all laughing.*
Brian *has gone off.*

Marion Eh come back you! I've not finished wi' you!

Carol *and* **Louise** *pass* **Scullery**.

Scullery Hey I'm on special offer; don't miss your bargain,
girls.

Carol *and* **Louise** *look at each other, smile, grab the trolley and
shove him off.*

Scullery (*as he goes*) OOOhhhhhhhhhhhhhhhhhhhh.

Blackout.

In the Royal Court production:

Bald and **Mrs Bald** were played by one actor doing two
voices.

In the **Eddie** and **Dad** scene (page 17), **Eddie** had his own
cassette player and throughout the beginning of the scene
an unspoken battle ensued with **Eddie** turning the cassette
volume up and **Dad** turning the television volume higher,
etc.

On **Barry**'s entrance with the pool cue (page 56), he involved
one of the audience in a mock game.

Glossary

turns – stage acts
reet – right
summat – something
owt – anything
nowt – nothing
snog – passionate kiss
immersion – heater for hot water
nutted – head butted
tab – cigarette
knacked – exhausted
one-armed combat – unarmed combat (Malapropism)
Giro – unemployment cheque
butty – sandwich
jack on – erection
skrike – cry
whome – home

Bed

Bed was first performed at the National Theatre on 8 March 1989 with the following cast:

Captain	John Boswell
Charles	Charles Simon
Sermon Head	Graham Crowden
The Couple	Donald Bisset and Joan White
Marjorie	Margery Withers
Spinster	Vivienne Burgess
Bosom Lady	Ruth Kettlewell

Director	Julia Bardsley
Designer	Peter J. Davison
Lighting	Christopher Toulmin
Music	John Winfield

In the half light we see a bedroom with a big bed, 30ft wide or more, almost covering the stage. Up one side of the room a mountain of armchairs and a massive window and curtains. Up the other side a chest of drawers mountain and, high on the wall, a little wooden cabinet upside down.

Directly over the bed is a shelf, on which are many bedtime things covered in dust: books, bottle and spoon, broken alarm clock etc. and a thing which looks like a head or bust but is not too clear in the half dark.

We hear breathing.

Lights come up further and we are aware of seven elderly people lying in bed.

Bosom Lady I'm too warm.

Captain I'm boiling.

Charles I'm boiled.

Spinster We've all got our aches and pains.

Marjorie On the edge of sleep.

Bosom Lady Toffee eyes.

Captain I love sleeping but I can never get deep like the old days.

The Couple We share it.

Charles I suck on sleep like a boiled sweet.

Spinster Speaking of boiled, I am.

Marjorie Moon-calf. Moon-calf.

Bosom Lady Asleep in the ooze.

Bosom Lady *pulls a biscuit out of her cleavage, nibbles it.*

Charles Pass the biscuit.

Spinster Gum the crumbs.

Marjorie Mattress of bread.

Bosom Lady Well, we're all toasting it then.

Captain Speak up, I can't hear over here.

Charles No one's 'spose to, it's sleep time.

Spinster I wish I could. I wish I could. Not even a pill can help.

Marjorie Count sheep.

Captain Count sheep's arses.

Bosom Lady You old toothless dirty mouth.

Charles Shave sheep and sleep in the wool coils.

Spinster I could 'cause I always knit sleep round me.

Marjorie It is a slow thing coming I'll grant you.

Bosom Lady It takes its time.

The Couple We save sleep up.

Charles When I close my eyes, where am I? When I open them, where?

Spinster When I close my eyes, all sorts drop. When I open them after that the dark's all in pieces.

Marjorie It's like black sand when it shifts.

Bosom Lady Heavy on your chest.

Captain Pressing your breaths.

Charles I'm telepathic.

Spinster The mattress has me now.

Charles I know.

Bosom Lady Give up the ghost.

Captain (*looking under the blankets*) When you think how underwear's changed through the ages.

Charles God I wish I was under the sea, a sea sleep.

Spinster Sea-rious.

Marjorie He certainly is.

Bosom Lady My dreams are silent movies.

Captain Give us the snore song someone.

Charles I dream westerns.

The Couple We dream in time.

Spinster Who are we, where do we go?

Marjorie Cuddle me. Cuddle me.

Captain Are there refreshments.

Charles Shall we pray.

Bosom Lady (*beginning to drift off again*) Dreaming again. Folding and unfolding white again.

Charles (*going also*) A shower of feathers and snow.

Spinster (*brushes mattress as she goes*) Sugar in the bed.

They are all beginning to fall.

Bosom Lady We all lie back and just whisp away.

Back to sleep.

Long pause.

Charles *suddenly sits bolt upright.*

Charles I'm off. I put my driving hat on. (*Takes trilby out from under sheets, puts it on.*) Turn the key. Over the kerb. Nice sound underneath. Round the village pond. (*Leans into it as he goes. Waves to someone.*) Hello. Steady now over the bumps and holes. Bloody things! (*Sees someone.*) Morning Vicar. Yes splendid. Oh dear. (*Changes gear.*) Up the wee brew. Come on you can do it girl. Stop at the top.

Bosom Lady *suddenly comes up beside him with a basket on her arm.*

Bosom Lady Hello.

Charles (*surprised*) Oh.

Bosom Lady Could you just stop at the bottom shop so I can buy some strawberry jam again.

Charles Okay. But hold on tight. (*Lets brake go.*) Because here we go!

They shoot down the hill.

Bosom Lady Whooooooooooooooooooooooooo.

Charles Ha harrrrrrrrrr.

They stop at the bottom.

Bosom Lady Won't be a mo.

Charles I'll leave the engine running.

She's gone under the covers.

Captain Psss.

Charles *looks round.*

Captain It's me old boy. Going far?

Charles Could be, not sure yet.

Captain Mind if I join you?

Charles I er . . . . . .

Captain (*clinks bottles under the blankets*) I've a few fresh stout here. (*Clinks again.*)

Charles (*friendly*) Clamber in old chap, there's a rug at the back, slip them under.

He lifts **Charles'** *pillow to slip them behind.*

Captain What's this, white chicken and ham. A beautiful cheese. An apple pie.

Charles Shush. Sh. Sh.

Suddenly everyone's up and sniffing in their sleep, following their noses.

Bosom Lady (*comes back with shopping*) Strawberries, chocolate cake, spam.

At this **Marjorie** *and* **Spinster** *and* **The Couple** *clamber in on each side behind* **Charles.** **The Couple** *though sitting up remain asleep. In front,* **Captain** *is one side of* **Charles, Bosom Lady** *the other.*

Spinster
Marjorie } Are we off then?

Charles (*with a car full, giving in*) Oh werry vell. Werry vell.

Captain Come on the anchors away!

Spinster
Marjorie } Yes yes.
Bosom Lady

Marjorie Foot well down. (**Charles** *presses his horn.*) PEEP PEEP!

Spinster Wheels free.

They all shudder forward.

Marjorie We're off!

They move as though travelling. All happy.

Charles The tickle belly bridge.

They bump over it.

All Wooooooooooooooo. (*Laughter.*)

Charles Down the tree lined.

They all press forward.

And out, out into the open road.

Spinster (*leans over*) Not so fast Charles. Faster!

She giggles.

Bosom Lady Yes race him. (*A passing car.*) Oh he's gone.

Charles Has he.

He suddenly changes gear. They all make the sound of the car as they surge forward. Wind blasted. Racing. They pass the other car. They all cheer. Wave. Pull faces. Blow raspberries. Blow kisses. As they pass.

Charles (*proud*) Here we go!

At the back they begin sharing out the food and beer.

– Anyone like a

– Lovely.

– Anyone like a

– Lovely.

– Anyone.

– Lovely.

– Anyone like a.

Charles Don't forget your driver.

Bosom Lady Here we go. Chicken leg one side.

He takes a bite, as she holds it.

Marjorie Beer the other. (*She pours some in his mouth.*)

They drive and eat.

Charles Look at that. Trees and then the lake. Trees and then the lake and the sun sliced on it.

Bosom Lady Oh I love this way round.

Marjorie The sun's making the road sparkle.

Spinster You feel as though you can catch things as you pass.

Bosom Lady *makes to catch something.*

Spinster What's that?

Bosom Lady A leaf.

Marjorie *catches something.*

Spinster What's that?

Marjorie A little bird. (*Lets it go.*) There she goes.

The women all blow a kiss.

Captain *catches something.*

Spinster What's that?

Captain Some litter. (*Undoes the crumpled paper a bit.*) No a poem. England . . .

Charles *begins to say it. As he does, they all settle back down to sleep.* **Captain** *with the paper over his face.* **Charles** *continues out.*

Charles England you summer beast. You humped bridges, you singing streams, you bumble hum, you round the cottage door. England you waxy rose. You scent. You hay stem in the mouth. You peasant-backed, rich-fronted, meadows and cheese and slow turn place. England you bowler hat/crown. You English Englishness English England. You green thing. You shape. You British school of motoring. You decent breakfast. You lived in land. You and your deep green indented green covered parts. Your cities sprung and crooked and sooted and historical. Stone England. Lassie and Laddie and Lord Land. You're pinched up in places and flattened in others, you have pubs and crannies and nooks, woods and brooks, fag end and piss precincts and towns of seventies cement, and modern, the word modern. And little birds lost and coughing. And motorways strapped across the fat of your land. Dark black, lit yellow. Cars come under the lights and the bridges and inside the automobiles people's heads are buzzing, they are. There's noises that have built up over the past thirty years, new and not right and in front and behind, and the brains gone puff ball, or modernly cooked, micro chumped. Beamed. Sucky. Not to be held. Past the sell-by date. Modern man has always just eaten. He's yellowed and flabby ripe. He's useless, killable. Standing in his underpants in the middle of the motorway with a personal hi-fi on.

Charles ⎫
Captain ⎬ Screaming his bloody balls off.

Charles There's no more room in England any more for a Tra lu lu lal lal lah.

Captain *lets the paper go out the window.*

Bosom Lady I sometimes think that, and I think what a hard day's night.

They all sing the Beatles' song 'A Hard Day's Night' as they drive.

Charles Life on the open road.

Marjorie Where we going this night?

They all freeze. The lights go.

Charles You shouldn't have said night, it's gone dark now.

Bosom Lady Oh it's pitch black.

Charles Hang on. (*Makes a cluck sound with his mouth. Two of them turn on little torches under the sheet and hold them one each side as headlights.*)

They begin to travel again slowly. Slowly.

Spinster Don't go too fast down here Charles.

Bosom Lady What's that noise?

Marjorie Are there ghosts?

Captain Don't ask me, ask outside.

Bosom Lady (*looking out*) The leaves have gone black leather.

Spinster Wet too.

Marjorie It'll rain next.

Charles Watch what you say. Watch what you say.

Spinster Where are we?

Charles Is there no map?

Bosom Lady No.

Captain Yes. (*He lets the sheet crumple across his lap like a relief map and follows the folds and contours with his finger.*)

Charles We're just passing some black tucked in and shining.

Captain (*following map*) Yes yes.

Bosom Lady And a hazy dark a bit shut.

Captain (*still following the signs*) Yes yes.

Marjorie And some tall night tight, no swollen.

Captain Yes yes.

Spinster Then a corner offered. Then taken back.

Captain Yes yes.

Bosom Lady Some flittery shade.

Captain Right then! Just take the next, and there it is, a bright house of refreshment.

Marjorie Not ghosts?

Captain Not according to this.

She kisses him.

They all lean as though taking a big corner.

Charles And here we are.

To the left of them appears an area of bright light.

They go a little apprehensive again as **Charles** *stands up and walks slowly over the bed and looks into the space of light, then turns back towards them.*

Charles It's a damn disco. Come on in.

They all cross the bed and into the light, happy. They cram into the space of light. It's pleasant. They are dancing, dancing. Lights dim on them. Suddenly the head on the shelf opens its mouth and speaks.

Sermon Head
Here I am!
I'm here!
The constantly awake,
never slept,
shelved but
ever seeing,
spying my chances
with my raw eye (*Opens it wider, burning red.*)
and his partner, 'Eaten'. (*Opens other, the same.*)
To cock up your kip.
All I've got, my
eyes, mouth, spittle,
skin, all of me, 'Why not take all of me'

You wouldn't would you? Would you.
You have to.
All of me
sheds out irritation
by the night-cap full
I shed irritation all through
till dawn
and I shed it with glee
with night-twisting glee.
I savour any wakings I can cause in them.
I savour every one.
They're all that keep me
going in here, in this 'all-I've-got' head. (*Eyes shut, shaking his
head about, as though trying to get out.*)
Head! Head! Head!
Sleep doesn't want me.
Did I tell you.
Arrrrrrrrrrrrrrrrrrrrrrrrrrrrrrrrrhhh !
(*Half shouted, sung, at top pitch.*)
UH CHU CHU CHEE!
UH CHEE CHU CHEE CHU CHU!
UH CHU CHU CHEE!
UH CHEE CHU CHEE CHU CHU!
UH CHU CHU CHEE . . .

*This disturbs the dancers. Lights dim on him and up on dancers,
who are very disturbed now by the noise. They dance on but
uncomfortable now. The disco seems crowded. The atmosphere has
become unpleasant. They get nasty with each other. They argue
bunched tightly together moving across the bed, still in the space of
light and its boundaries, moving, the light going with them.*

Sermon Head *stops singing, his purpose accomplished. They break
and all return to bed, sitting up in bed now in a glum row. (Except*
The Couple *who have gone to sleep.) Still angry with each other.*

Throughout the following speech, they begin to doze off again.

Sermon Head As you can imagine I've made a life long
study of sleep. I've become what you might call
obsessional and snoozle fanatical. But 'tis pure academical
and leaves me still distanced from that one article, of my
desire, sleep. Oh sleep, sleep sweet roller, kiss the inside of

Sermon Head's lids and let me fall into thee. (*Closes his eyes.
Opens them.*) Why not, eh? WHERE IS MY SHARE? Oh stop
it Sermon Head grab yourself together. Hold your head up.
Look the night right in the eye. (*He does, his eyes wide open,
burning raw red.*) Look with these raging balls and sawn off
sockets. Open. There. Bam. Bam.

Suddenly from sleep all of them.

All Shut up Sermon Head!

Sermon Head Oh now we have it. Here they come as usual.
Sympathy, whatever happened to it? They're at me again.
Taunters. Mattress yobs.

They shout. Throw things at him.

Charles Pipe down!

Sermon Head I can't wear pyjamas!

Spinster Close it!

Couple Sssssssssssssh.

Sermon Head I've never stretched!

Marjorie Oh stop.

Captain Shut the trap.

Charles Quit while you're a head.

They all laugh.

Sermon Head Oh very funny.

Spinster (*mocking*) He can't ever sleep.

Sermon Head I can so. I'm just on a sleep diet that's all.

They laugh.

Sleep fats!

They ignore him.

I'll get you lot and I bloody well will. Oh yes snore on.
Snore on. . . . . .

They all settle back to sleep.

I'll have a go at them. I hate them. They keep their sleep in the bank. Full vaults or overdrawn up the nostrils. Well I want 'em wakened. I wish there were more ways available to me. Wish I was a Thermostat Face, red cheek gauged. Then I could chill or could concentrate up a heat, could bake their little throats. Look at those throats all in a row like beige sausage. Like sausage rolls. Crisp up throats, crack and buckle, flake. (*He blows dust from off the shelf onto them.*)

Marjorie *gives a cough.*

Got one anyway.

Marjorie (*waking*) So thirsty oh I'm dry.

No reply.

Oh I can't sleep for it.

Captain Don't worry there. Get your head under the ocean like me.

Marjorie I'll try. So sorry all.

Spinster What is it?

Bosom Lady Her little throat keeps telling her.

Charles Halt the breath between your lips. Sip it right down then start again.

Bosom Lady Is that what you do. You genius.

Marjorie Oh so thirsty.

Bosom Lady Use your spit dear.

Sermon Head *laughs.*

Spinster Think of water.

Captain Yes sink of water.

Couple Don't mention the stuff. It makes it worse.

Charles Clunk your tongue round, there might be some juice left.

Sermon Head *laughs.*

Bosom Lady Water! Water! Water to do!

Captain I'm tucking in the waves all round, nice and cosy and splashy.

Marjorie So thirsty it's hurting.

Spinster Ssssssssh you're starting me off now.

Couple Sufferings sufferings.

Sermon Head Belt up and bring her a glass of water for sleepssake!

Silence. They are all still but with eyes wide open, tense. Pause.

Couple (*slowly*) We'll go for the glass of water.

Marjorie Thank you so very much. How can I ever . . .

All of them begin pulling back the blankets and sheets industriously, busy doing their different tasks like a trained crew. The blankets are rolled back. Pillows mounted. Covers untucked. Sheets tied and knotted etc. **The Couple** *during this are putting on their dressing-gowns and slippers. The others proceed to the bed centre on all fours or knees, and ease up and ease out and ease up then suddenly out a perfect round shape of mattress, a clear lid. The slices of sheet and spring are very visible at the side like a piece of cake. And as it leaves the hole a beam of light shoots right up strong to the ceiling. They then proceed to lower* **The Couple** *down the hole by the knotted sheets. When they are out of sight they solemnly close the lid, restore the sheets etc. and silently return to bed. Then to sleep.*

Sermon Head I'm still awake. I have to mention it. You see how I had them, worried, well wakened. Staring into the light, like me. And now they're right back where we started. Sleep's too magnetic in its drawing. Won't drag me off into its dark suck though will it. Oh, you leave me so jealous! You sleep easies – You yawn friends. Slumber dogs. Doing your greed sleeping. Snoring. Lip fluttering under the covers and blankets, wool and cotton all over your mouths. Breath swopping. Look at you all in your dream wigs.

They wake.

Bosom Lady Shut up Sermon Head.

Captain Get slept.

Sermon Head Look at you in that lovely big bed, you're not worthy of it. When I think of the bed my poor Mother headed. A dirty bed. A 'kicked' bed. Squeaking in its hundred voices, the stinking square. Always moving. A corner torn off. Full of old hands and the soft sinky breasts of Victorian chars . . .

Charles Shut him up, someone.

Spinster Give him the poke.

One of them quickly pulls from under the bed a very long duster, (as long as it needs to be to reach him) sharp end first, and using this end pokes him right in the cheek with it. He starts squealing at top pitch. They poke him again. He shuts up. The duster is returned. They turn over and sleep.

Blackout.

Lights up on **The Couple,** *who are half-way up and still scaling the armchair mountain. They stop and rest in a couple of the chairs.*

Woman To

Man gether.

Woman Tied.

They kick off and the armchairs suddenly swing out and very gently go back and forth out over the bed like swings.

Woman Shared.

Man We've shared ourselves away to each other.

Woman I'd give you my air and you'd return it with yours.

Man Do we still love we.

Woman It is love but we're making it last. Are we happy?

Man I've forgotten. Did you put the cat out?

Woman Twenty years ago.

Man And it never came back the swine.

Both
One hand, one wrist, one arm. Our minds
have faded together.
Our souls are hugging.
There's only a second betwixt our hearts beats
enough just for separation.
They go
  we're two no one
    two one
  we're two no one
    two one.

Both (*sing*)
We are the kinder things of life
We place our breaths
We're in the air almost

Man We're done in watercolours.

Woman Our hearts go like rocking chairs.

Sermon Head What about the glass of water, you stupid old
sods!

They remember, park up the armchairs and hurry away.

He turns his attention to those below, still smarting from poke.

(*Whispering.*) I'll give you all sore pillows, sore pillows I will.
I'll make that a sick bed I will, I'll . . .

Someone turns over below. He goes quiet.

(*Looking at them all sleeping.*) You sod gums. You . . . Just
look at them. I hate that. They'll hate this. Well one will. (*He
starts to laugh. He gently and softly sings an old sea shanty.*)

This disturbs **Captain**. *He begins tossing and turning, thrashing
the bed-clothes. Pulling them off the others. They all pull them back.
He pulls them off. They pull them back.*

Captain (*in sleep*) No. Hold. Don't falter. Lash. Criss cross.
Send it back overboard, fill your palms with the salty stuff
and throw. Sea leave me!

He seems to settle again. Then **Sermon Head** *very softly and low* *sings a little more of the sea shanty. (Throughout this speech a great storm builds, the window blows open and a powerful gale thrashes the curtains. The others huddle in their sleep.)*

Oh not again. You blaster. I've washed tonight, I've brushed my reef. Oh no here I go. I'm up. I'm down. Hold me someone. It's raging again. The storm. All my belongings are out on the deck, travelling, like swimming sheep following each other over the side, drank away. Skidding books, wet, slapped on the wood, gone. The rains bouncing feets high. I'm going to hold on. Oh yes I am. I'm going to hold. Trapped between two ragers, the sky and the sea, hopelessly caught in the zig-zag between. We're high then low. Bouncing. Sometimes suspended a second, in so much noise it's like silence. Then flung down again. Spun and slanted by the sea. It can't bear us on its surface. There's a dead dog on the deck, *(The ladies scream, then back to sleep.)* spinning around and around in the skud, then gone. I shall hold. Oh I shall hold. It's gathering now all of it and I'm in the mid. I'm waiting. I'm holding. I'm gripping on, arms around the mast. My legs sea-logged, thrown about. I've bitten my lip off, it came away like wet paper. I'm biting my bite now. Thoughts won't stay, my mind's slid. I'm cold, numb, slub. There's my will. I can see it before my eyes. A cannon barrel. Hold. Pray hold. And you and you and you. I wish you were here now. And she, where's gone, where's gone . . . Pray from right under. Pray deep under. Pray over. Pray over. Praysa! Praysa! *(Lets out an almighty cry.)* Grarrrrrrrrrrrrrrrrrrrrrrrrrrrrrrrrrrrrrrrrrrrrrrrrrrrrrrrrrrrrr! *(Suddenly, looking high and around, still standing, arms out, as though in the air. Startled, wonder-struck.)* Now I'm in a great and total circle of sea. Now thrown. But it's like flying. *(Goes down.)* Suddenly I'm in the water, supported. *(Lies down in stages.)* It's like a chair, now a plank, now wet cloth. Now my limbs are spread and free, sea-surrounded, it's hurrying to fit all my outside spaces, between my arms and body, between my legs. Warm salt waters. Lulled, passed from wave to wave. Then a seagull, the cliffs and headboard. I'm back washed up on the bed. Pillow-shored. Glad to be alive. Sea-gargled. Calm.

All their breaths and snoring become that of a calm sea off a shore.

The wind has died away. But the window is still open. **The Couple** *are perched on the window sill. Still shaken by the storm and clutching onto each other. They close the window.*

Woman (*afraid*) Oh dear.

Man Which way is it now?

Woman It's going on a long time. Are you shaking?

Man Yes I quite am.

Woman So am I.

Man I have to put your hair back it's all over the place.

He begins to do this.

Woman (*for comfort*) Bring your face close. Closer, I don't want to see it all in one go. But closer still. I want to read a little to comfort me. Our times together have turned the skin, made beautiful lines.

Man I'm still in your hair.

Woman Where did your face come from?

Man *shakes his head, still sorting her hair out.*

Woman (*she is silently going over his face, touches a mark on his skin*) Who put that there? (*Silence as she continues looking over face, closer.*) I go from one true story to another. In your smooth skin, shades, foldage and lines, I see the all of us. I . . . Closer. Close. Closer still. (*They grip tightly in an embrace.*)

Light fades off them and up on **Sermon Head.**

Sermon Head (*glares down at the sleepers*) Zedding hogs. Sleep sippers and spitters. Look at 'em cooking in their own snoring heat. One nose after another. Oh but really and truly what could be better than a night in bed. You cannot get a good English sleep these days. I can't even get a takeaway. They're not worthy of sleep them snore hogs. I am. So am. Number one sleep fan, student, swot. I've grasped all its degrees, I've got Forty Winks after me name. I've classified every type. One's sleep is well used. Another second hand. One's is brittle. One's is see-through. One's is alchemical. One's is passed around. One's a sleepskin rug. One's ladling sleep from a bucket. One has the bonfire smell. One's is bread hot. One's is very wrong. One's is clot. One's is like hands in beautiful hair. There's all these sleep sorts and more, oh yes more. But none come near Sermon Head, I can't even get a thin thread of it. It's just not me. Doesn't go with my eyes.

Stops. Then starts forming crossword words.

One down
Two, two across
Four down
Three.

Charles (*in sleep*) Three up.

Captain (*in sleep*) Two across.

Marjorie (*in sleep*) One down.

Captain How many letters?

Charles *awakes, gets his newspaper and pen out. Sits up. Starts doing the crossword.*

Spinster (*in sleep*) Yes I'm feeling better.

Bosom Lady (*in sleep*) Are you?

Captain Two was it two?

Charles No it was five.

Marjorie Is there a 'C'?

Captain I've just been in the sea.

Bosom Lady Was it five?

Captain No, one in it?

Marjorie That's me, I'll knit. (*She awakes, gets her knitting, Sits up.*)

Bosom Lady Who' won it?

Captain Is there an 'I' in it?

Spinster I'll iron it. (*Sits up, still in sleep. Starts smoothing pillow*) I have to.

Charles No, there was an 'S' in it.

Bosom Lady S . . O . .

Captain I'll take four Gallions.

Charles He's back in the bloody sea.

Captain Aye aye.

Bosom Lady 'I' in it.

Spinster I am ironing it!

Bosom Lady Sure there was an 'O' in it.

Captain One or two 'O's in it. Toes in it. (*He awakes, sits up to clip his toes.*)

Charles 'C' . . .

Marjorie Who do you see?

Bosom Lady (*awakes, sitting up, looking in hand mirror*) Me.

Charles 'D' that's it
D.I.S.C.O.
Disco!

He fills it in.

Spinster *awakes, stands indicating the mess the bed is in after the storm.*

Spinster
Ahhh this I can no longer abide.
Neither should they.
Chaos, a roughed den in which sin can hide.
With vigour my hands shake it out.
I rawl disorder.
And I can go a choking in the thrown about.

She grabs a pile of sheets and blankets as though throttling them, and throws them straight. She continues moving over the bed, restoring it.

Even in my birth I
nipped singularly all my
Mother's side
I came out clean, not covered in blood,

a matron slide.
Since then it has always been my way,
Scouring life.
Setting standards that never stray.
(*She suddenly strokes the darkness itself.*)
The night itself I like a good black.
As from old cross or kettle
Coated back
Edwardian metal
Not too lit upon.
Rubbed or seared
to the dark of my religion.

She tries to move the blankets from **Bosom Lady** *who won't let her.*
Spinster *punches her hard in her big arm.* **Bosom Lady** *howls.*
She hits her again on the exact same spot.

Charles   Hey steady on!

Marjorie   Leave her be!

Captain   Hey!

She spins to face them arms upraised in a terrifying gesture of kill.
Hands clasped over her head, holds it, shaking shaking with anger.
Bosom Lady *moves for her. Then she brings clasped hands over to*
a kind of praying position in front of her chest, then lets them go.
And continues tidying as though nothing had happened.

Spinster
Strangely I find that in place of love, hate
is often the best
cleaning agent
to penetrate and separate.
(*Continues her work.*)
My body has kept well. Kept out of sight.
My breast bared
to no babe or light (*She touches her breasts.*)
Two sheet corners sharpened
squeezed only by age
Milkless and whitened
Bit beaten with rage.

Sermon Head   Shut up you old bag!

Spinster *reaches under bed, pulls out feather duster, sharp end first.* **Sermon Head** *starts screaming. Then she turns it round to the, big feathered side of the duster. He sighs with relief. She reaches up with it and briskly knocks him off the shelf. The head falls screaming to the bed. In his sleep* **Charles** *puts it under a pillow to quiet it.* **Spinster** *continues making bed.*

Spinster
This our country needs remaking
As I remake this
Its foundations are flaking
Its spirit misshapen
There's a smell rising
From where our tradition has been forsaken
It's under beds and off the shore
Putrification.
England hangs off the map
half scrounger, half whore.
Oh Britannia,
doing anything to get fat.
Morally sparse.
Fast-fingered heathens steal her crown
while mauling her arse.

She has almost finished off the tucking in. It is much too tight over them. Tucked in so tight they can hardly breathe.

As I turn back the covers
straight-lined
I also turn back my mind
to my memories, mainly
neatly stacked ashes. (*Her mood changes.*)
Save that one, the one
Where the wind over the moor dashes.
An almighty wind
Apostles in the grasses,
Cloistered trees unbound,
Sky and clod earth
shoving out the cathedral sound.
A young me there, thumping
with nature
Hymns all over my hair,
a Bible picture.

She stops herself and squeezes under tight sheets.

My life's a commandment
and in it I'm entrenched
My heart feels like a giant
silent choir clenched.
Wants to sing
after all these years,
But I've tightened it in
with ribs and fears.
Many other inner organs
are the same way gagged.
Bitterness runneth over
But love on the sharp ends
of my bigoted bones gets snagged.
(*Getting the line of the sheet under her chin just right.*)
You see I have to do my right
Keep account.
Perfect nib must be
lifted clean from page each night.
My life ledger *will be in order*
I shall not be shook off.
I have my teeth and
claws, in my God's cold shoulder.

She looks out. She looks up with just her eyes.

(*Under her breath, hard.*) Turn that light out.

Blackout.

The **Couple Man** *in a corner by himself, her slipper in his hand. Lost.*

Man I am lost. We have got somehow separated. It's cold on own. My breathing's gone all funny. There's dark everywhere. (*He looks around.*) Is this loneliness? (*Pause.*) How did I get here? I can't remember. She looked after the memory. (*Pause.*) Was I dreaming her all these years? (*Looks at slipper.*) Oh my dearest, I have your smell and fluff, but you you.

Suddenly three little cries come, almost like a phone ringing. It is coming from the slipper. He puts it to his ear.

Hello.

Lights come up on **Woman***. She has the other slipper at her ear. Talks into it.*

Woman Who is this please?

Man Is that you?

Woman Yes. Is that you?

Man Yes.

Woman Are we found?

Man We are. Are you all right, my dearest?

Woman I'm not bloody sure. Are you all right?

Man Yes. Would you care for a night stroll?

Woman Very well.

They put down the slippers and begin whistling as they walk to meet at the bed corner. She slips on her slippers then links with him. They set off pleasantly strolling.

This is a good way.

Man Yes.

Woman This corner's tricky.

Man (*agreeing*) Uh, uh.

They walk on.

Woman Are we on a sleepwalk?

Man No.

Woman Well, why aren't we in bed then?

Both (*remembering*) The glass of water!

Man It's here somewhere.

Woman There's not many places left.

They reach the drawers. They look at them. She opens bottom drawer. Searches one side.

Not in here.

He searches the other side.

Man No no.

Woman A vest. Whose is this vest?

Man (*as he moves on to next drawer*) We'll never know.

They search.

Not in here.

Woman She's depending on us.

As she passes to next drawer.

Man She is.

As he joins her at drawer.

Both We mustn't fail now.

They search.

Man Not here.

Both Where then?

Woman *looks up.* **Man** *follows the look. They see the cabinet high on the wall. They look at each other in acknowledgement.*

Man *begins to climb the drawers they have left out, as though they were a staircase.* **Woman** *holds his dressing-gown cord as he ascends. He climbs high until he reaches a level with the cabinet. He leans out and can just reach it. He manages to open it. And then things, things multitudinous come pouring, pouring out for a long, long time. It seems they will never stop. Then suddenly it is empty and we see just a glass left, but upside down on the shelf, empty, a thin light cutting through it, making it glint in its emptiness.* **Man** *reaches up for it and takes it out.*

Both Empty empty empty.

They begin to weep. This wakens **Spinster** *who gets up. She notices at the bed corner a bit of sheet sticks out; she crawls over to it, she tugs it, tugs it back, then peels it right back off the corner.*

*Underneath is soft black soil. She takes from under the bed a big
spade and digs into the earth, digs again. The sound wakes the
sleepers, who stand and step forward in a straight line facing the
audience.* **Spinster** *begins to rake through the soil with her hands.
She finds a small plaque on old wood. She passes it to* **Bosom
Lady** *who passes it to* **Charles** *who passes it to* **Marjorie** *who
passes it to* **Captain.** **Captain** *instantly breaks into tears at the
sight of it.* **Spinster** *rakes up more, finds a little baby's shoe. She
passes to* **Bosom Lady** *who passes to* **Charles** *who passes to*
Marjorie. **Marjorie** *bursts into tears.* **Spinster** *rakes on, she finds
a letter, she passes to* **Bosom Lady** *who passes to* **Charles** *who
bursts into tears. She finds a photograph. She passes to* **Bosom
Lady** *who immediately cries. She rakes more. She finds a little lace
handkerchief, she begins crying herself at this, and then into it. The
others gather around the patch of earth as though at a grave side
and slowly let their objects fall back into the earth, still weeping.*
Spinster *passes the handkerchief up to the others and they each dry
their tears with it as she again buries the past. The hanky reaches*
Bosom Lady *last, she dries her tears then sees* **The Couple**
*are crying too and passes it up to them. They cry into it. Spinster has
re-covered the earth and then, along with the others, returns to bed
and sleep.* **The Couple** *cry into the handkerchief. It is so wet* **Woman**
*wrings it out. It begins filling the glass. They are overjoyed. Happy.
they start laughing.*

Lights fade on them.

Lights up on **Bosom Lady** *who has caught the laughter and is
giggling in her sleep. She suddenly wakens and sits up laughing,
throwing from under the blankets, thousands of bras of all types
high into the air. They fall all over the bed.*

Bosom Lady How wonderful to just wake and bra around.

Suddenly **Sermon Head** *emerges from among the bras. One is
stuck over his face and he makes a muted complaint. She sees him,
removes the bra. . .*

Oh my Sermon.

*. . . and kisses him passionately all over his head and face, leaving
gigantic kiss marks. He is helpless in this to stop her, and screaming*

at top pitch. She covers his face with her bosom. We hear his muffled screaming. She takes her bosom away; he's still screaming. She puts it back over his face.

Awww dear, look in my medicine chest.

She takes it back. He is making a different sound now as though in shock, but still moaning. **Charles** *sits up, wraps a bra around* **Sermon Head**'s *face and fastens it at the back to shut him up.* **Bosom Lady** *starts kissing* **Charles.**

Charles Oh goodness gracious.

He disappears under the sheets. She turns out to the audience.

Bosom Lady In a way I am her Bosom majesty. Let me tell you, life has been just one long feather boa continually in the air! It has. If I look back along it I see one perfectly empty glass after another, and I can see in them the shimmering reflections of good food and cherries and chandeliers. I wouldn't know what 'stage' of life I am at now. But I do know when I exit through sleep, I make my entrance onto a little 'stage', lit through dusty bulbs and bedside lamps. Some nights there's a Berlin cabaret on, or a circus, a Can-Can, or my favourite, an English Music Hall, with a good all round bill of healthy entertainment.

Sermon Head *squeaks, squeaks, behind the bra. She looks round at him.*

The comedy duo!

She goes back to **Sermon Head** *and undoes bra. He is gasping in air.*
(*As a comedian.*) I say, I say, why don't you face up to it and go to the party.

Sermon Head *mouth open, shaking his head, lost.*

I s'pose it is difficult when you've no*body* to go with.

Cymbals crash.

Every one a winner, every one a gem.
Oh that crazy stage. Sand dancers, fan dancers, acrobats, then me. Doing my speciality act 'The juggling of many bras'

or giving a song, a belter, or the other kind, dedicated to some man of mine. I take up my stance, my big armpits are sucking in and ready for whoosh, my big fluttery hands opening. And then there's music on the air, everywhere, a melody under the mattress, stray notes all over the bed, then rising, calling out to have a song flown on them.

Sings the Rogers and Hart song 'Dancing On The Ceiling'.

After the first verse **Sermon Head** *joins her in singing the rest of the song, as they all go through a dance routine, based on sleep movements etc. while still lying in bed. It ends. They return to sleep.*

Blackout.

Pin light on **Sermon Head.**

Sermon Head Sermon Head in bed. I've made it. But really what a waste. Beaten, ravaged, yet still unrested. Even in such a bed as this, sleep can resist me. I give up. I give up everything. I give up even the trying. (*Depressed, silent.*) Wait something's happening. My eyes they're going. Jaw too. I'm slipping little inside. Look at me nodding. (*Head nods.*) Can, can this be sleep at long, long last. (*As he speaks this his head is lowering towards mattress.*)

Just as his cheek hits the delicious bed, **Captain** *lets out an enormous snore.* **Sermon Head** *springs back upright and awake.*

No.

Very angry now but no sound. He just bites into the sheets beside him, then spins upstage. This causes the sheets to be tugged slightly off the sleepers, disturbing them.

Marjorie *stands up in a sleepwalk way. The others stand too and link hands. As this is happening* **The Couple** *approach the bed with the glass of tears.* **Marjorie** *leads the others around the mattress to meet them. She stops, takes the drink, then carries on around the mattress and back to her place with everyone holding hands and following her in a long chain.* **The Couple** *catch on at the end and step back onto the bed.* **Marjorie** *picks up her pillow and crawls to sit on the extreme end of the bed holding it. The others gather up their pillows and scatter randomly all over the bed.*

They settle to sleep, clutching their pillows.

Marjorie Oh I. Well. Yes, yes.
We'd been married only a short time by then. He went in
the morning in the evening returned. Still clean. I had it
quiet and tidy for him. The clock ticking, he read the
newspaper up in front of his face, legs crossed, dark socks
on and long ankles. I'd sit and sometimes just look at his big
shoe hanging from the ankle. And he might lower the
newspaper and look over it at me staring, and I would start
as though waking from a dream and blush. And the blush
was always a cold blush, if you know what I mean. When I
served his dinner, the laying of the plate and the cutlery
always sounded out loud on the cloth, on our wedding table
under the window. I always had my hair up in a tight bun
then. And my style of clothes were the same, same as they
are now really, same as the house, as him, as his clothes and
socks. Which I wrung out through the wringer but these
were things that he never saw. He just saw the house as it
was when he left when he returned, Hello, pulling up his
trousers at the knee, sitting, the clock tick, the cloth, the
plate, the cutlery going down into the cloth, cruet, the pale
light coming through the netted curtains. The electric light
on in winter. He never really touched me, how can I say,
properly, once when my hair was slightly falling he pushed
it back up the neck, I felt two hard fingers there, they were
there for just a second too long, then gone. The personal
part of our life was like a jolt. I would taste his pyjamas in
my mouth from his shoulder. After he'd done with me he'd
lay back sweating a little, his eyes open then squeezed shut,
he didn't let the lids drop but squeezed them shut and slept
like that all night. It was maybe that night that it happened.
I told him quietly and he nodded quietly and said he was
pleased and it would be all right. And we telephoned his
sister in Bournemouth and both told her over the phone,
and she kept saying 'How loverly, well you two, well'. But
after that it was hardly mentioned. The front door would
go. The plate would go on the table. I'd see some dust on
the radio top and think how did I miss it. He'd step in and
the newspaper and the same. But it was all right because
within all this our baby was growing. Warm inside, glowing,

and it passed up to my face and my new chubby cheeks. (*She pinches them.*) When I started it was before he went to work luckily. And he ran me to the town hospital, took me in, left for work. I remember seeing his dark head pass the one two three windows. While I stood in my coat waiting to be seen by Sister, a nice woman, but such cracked hands. And as soon as she touched me I knew something was wrong inside, it felt cold, dead, hollow as though a draught was getting in and all I could think of was his boiled ham on the plate before the vegetables were placed round it and the clean white fat on the edge and his yellow mustard across the colours, horrible yellow, almost green and the meat too pink, unnatural, and unnatural, an unnatural shape. And the baby was dead when she came out, she was gone when she came out. And when he was told he nodded and when he was told he nodded. And later at home I did this (*A gesture, like holding a baby*) and later at home I did this and after that there were no more jolts in the night and after that we spoke even less and we stayed that way. And I didn't BLOODY CARE LOVE! And though it was winter and though I was still weak I went out into the garden in the snow and I threw my wish away.

Soft white feathers begin to fall in a shower. The others awaken. They lift their faces to it. **Sermon Head** *revolves to face front.* **Captain** *flicks snow off* **Marjorie**'s *hair and shoulders. The feather fall is very heavy now.* **Charles** *puts up a big brolly; they all come underneath it. The snow feathers falling. All of them, except* **Sermon Head**, *sing a lullaby ('Loo la bye bye'). It finishes.* **Charles** *slowly brings the brolly forward and down so that it covers them all from view. On it is written —*

GOOD NIGHT

Two

Two was first performed at the Bolton Octagon on
23 August 1989, with Sue Johnston and John McArdle
playing all the characters:

Landlord
Landlady
Old Woman
Moth
Maudie
Old Man
Mrs Iger
Mr Iger
Lesley
Roy
Fred
Alice
Woman
Little Boy

Directed by Andrew Hay
Designed by Mick Bearwish
Lighting by Phil Clarke

Note

The action takes place over one night, in a pub, in the
North of England.

Two is designed so that two people can play all the
characters. The set consists of a pub bar, with all glasses,
pumps, till, optics etc., being mimed as are the other
people in the pub to whom the actors relate. There are also
instances in the play where members of the audience may
be directly related to, if it is appropriate to the production.

The action should flow from one scene to the next
without a break, therefore costumes should be minimal.

Blackness. Suddenly, lights up on **Landlord** *and* **Landlady** *behind bar working and serving.*

Landlord There you go love, two pints. Tar.

Landlady What was it now? Babycham and two Appletisers.

Landlord And now sir, a pint and a half of lager.

Landlady It was a Babycham wasn't it?

Landlord (*from mouth corner*) Get it together.

Landlady Sod off. (*To customer.*) There you go dear.

Landlord Thanks. And what's your poison? (*To someone else.*) Be with you in a minute.

Landlady Tar. Nice to see you two back together again. Yes.

Landlord (*while serving*) Er, can you see to this lad here love?

Landlady (*still to customer*) Right lovey, see ya. (*To* **Landlord**.) Eh?

Landlord Here love, customers, thirsty. (*Under breath.*) Move it woman.

Landlady Stuff it man. (*To customer.*) Yes love can I help you?

Landlord Right then, with ice was it?

Landlady Sorry, no cherries.

Landlord (*to* **Landlady**) What's them down there, blind arse.

Landlady You'll have a' lager instead, okay. (*To* **Landlord**.) Don't get smart with me Pigoh.

Landlord Uh. There you go now. Thanks.

Landlady (*to someone leaving*) See you. What? Oooooooooh.

Landlord (*glares at her, then to customer*) Nice to see you, what's it to be? White wine and a Barbican.

Landlady Two double Drambuies, well well. Where the hell is that now?

Landlord There! There! (*Realises he's shouting and laughs back at customers. To* **Landlady**.) You'll be the death of me.

Landlady If only, if only.

Landlord Get damn serving.

Landlady I am. I am, if you'll keep your poxy nose out.

Landlord (*to customer*) Oh sorry. What was it again?

Landlady (*she cracks up laughing at this, he gives her a black look. To customer*) Two double Drambuies for you.

Landlord White wine and a Barbican. Not in the same glass I hope, ha!

Landlady (*at joke*) Oh my God. (*Serves customer.*) There you go loves. Tar.

Landlord Love, can you just reach me a Barbican from down there.

Landlady Where? Oh yes.

She crouches down for it. He quickly goes down too. They are both out of view.

Landlady Ow.

Landlord (*comes up*) Here we are.

Landlady (*comes up, rubbing her side*) Little swine. Ow. I'll get you for that. (*To customer at bar.*) Yes. Ah it's the happy couple. What would you like then?

Landlord So that's four Grolshes, two Buds, and a packet of peanuts.

Landlady Two sweet white wines, how nice. You didn't get much of a tan then.

Landlord There you go, your wish is my command.

Landlady There you go, on the house.

Landlord *spins round to glare.*

Landlady Well it was this very pub in which you met, wasn't it? Yes. Lovely, lovely. See you later.

Landlord (*to* **Landlady**) On the house. Lovely. Lovely. (*Suddenly realises couple are waving to him from their table.*) What? Oh congratulations. Awww, our pleasure.

Landlady Creep.

Landlord Crap.

Landlady Fart.

Landlord Hag.

Landlady (*steps over to a customer*) Two whiskeys was it? (*And straight over his foot.*)

Landlord Arrr. Ohh.

Landlady Oh dear, are you all right, love? He wants to take the weight off his feet, I keep telling him. Now then, two whiskeys.

Landlord (*distracted by customer*) A brandy and cider, right you are. Not in the same glass I hope. Ha.

Landlady *cringes.*

Landlady (*taking money*) 2.05 loves. Tar now.

Landlord There's your brandy, we'll soon have the cider beside her.

Landlady Painful. Painful.

Landlord It will be. It will be.

Landlady Sorry? (*Turns towards customer's voice.*) Oh it's you, how are you? I was wondering when you'd pop up.

Landlord 2.50 thanks. Lovely. (*To* **Landlady** *as she passes.*) Don't embarrass us, you look like his grandmum.

Landlady Do you want what you had last night? Oooooooh, you young wag. No serious though, what's your choice love? Okay. Well thanks I will. Thanks very, very much, you gallant young boy.

Landlord A Southern Comfort and crisps. (*He goes to get them.*)

Landlady (*to* **Landlord***'s customer*) If he says 'Not in the same glass', don't laugh please.

Landlord Not in the same glass, I hope?

Landlady (*laughs, then to her customer*) Now then sparrow, there you go, and tar, tar again. (*She winks.*)

Landlord Get out and get some glasses while it's quietening. Go on.

Landlady I'm going. I'm a going. (*She does.*)

He breathes out. Grabs up a cloth and starts wiping glasses.

Landlord (*turns to audience*) First night in here? Well, you'll get used to us. We're a lively pub. It's calmed down a bit now, but it comes in waves. Not going to ask you what you're doing here, never do, that's one of our few rules. We get a lot of rendezvousers here you see, but we're also strong on couples, don't get me wrong. They either come in pairs or end up that way. That woman over there is my wife, bitch. I run this place virtually on my own. We've been here bloody years. In fact we met outside this pub when we were kids, me and cow. Too young to get in, snotty conked, on tip-toes peeking through the frosted windows. We had our first drink in here, we courted in here, we had our twenty first's in here, we had our wedding reception here, and now we own the bloody place. I only did it for her, it's what she'd always wanted. Done some knocking through recently, got the walls down, made it all into one. You can get around better, and more eyes can meet across a crowded room. Better that, better for business and pleasure and for keeping an eye on that roving tart. Where is she with them glasses? Wouldn't mind a bloody drink meself, I'll have one later. It's a constant battle keeping your throat away from the stock. It

really is the landlord's last temptation. Because this is it
for us proprietors. This is our life, these bar sides, to them
wall sides and that's it. People and pints and measures
and rolling out the bloody barrel. Working and social life
all mixtured, a cocktail you can't get away from. Until
night when we fall knackered to bed. But I'm not
complaining, no, no. As long as many mouths are clacking
at many glasses and the tills keep on a singing. What more
could a publican want?

Old Woman *enters.*

Landlord Oh here she is, I can set the clock by this auld
dear. (*Puts glass under pump ready.*) Evening love, usual?

Old Woman Yes please, landlord.

Landlord How's everything love?

Old Woman Passing same. Passing sames.

Landlord Oh aye. There you go.

Old Woman Thank you, landlord.

Landlord Pleasure lovey. (*He goes.*) Where is she with
them bloody glasses?

He exits. She sips her drink. Then turns to the audience.

Old Woman Here I am at the end of my day. Taking my
reward from the glass. He's at home, he can't come out,
too crippled dear. But he allows me out for my drink at the
end of it all, the day. I've retired, but not really, 'cause
now I have to work twice as hard with him, lifting his
shitty bum off the blankets. He's having all the last bit of
my life, but I don't begrudge him that. Poor lumped man
he is, there he is at home, with his pint of dandelion and
burdock, watching the television in the dark. All's I do is
look after him and shop a lot, shop a lot with nowt.

Though I do like to go shopping, I like to, I like the
butcher best, blood everywhere, laughing his bloody head
off. He's fat too, fat. Fat like jelly pork. Pink. I love him,
though he doesn't know of course. It's his laughing that
does it, and his big butcher life, chopping and pulling
those beasts apart. Admirable. Me, myself, don't have
much strength left now, carrying my husband down the
stairs, I have to stop three times, my arms keep giving.
'Let's have our breather' I say, and we both stop, panting
like knackered cattle. I watch his chest going like the
clappers, and I watch mine going the same. And all our
wheezes echoing off the stairway and my swollen ankles,
and his watery eyes, and I wonder in God's starry heavens
why we keep going. We have each other, we have the
allowance, there's a lot of memories somewhere, there's a
bit of comfort in sleep and Guinness, but what the hell has
it all been about? I ask you. I carry him down. I carry him
up, piss all over my hands. His day, the tele-box. My day,
shopping bag. Butchers for a bit o' scrag, see him flipping
open the animals with his very sharp knife. Oh my day,
my life, my day, my drink here. Him at home with the
tele, in the burdock dark a dead dandelion in his mouth. I
can hear his old chest creaking from here, and on my neck
his chicken arms, chicken arms, and around my neck his
poorly chicken arms. Get me a Guinness. Stand me a
drink. Fetch the butcher with his slaughtering kit, may I
ask you all to raise your cleavers now please and finish the
job, raise them for the bewildered and pig weary couples
that have stuck, stuck it out. Thank you.

She bows her head as though to have it cut off.

Lights pick up **Moth** *chatting a young woman up. Imaginary or
real from the audience.* (*This scene may be performed in Liverpool
accents if desired.*)

Moth You're beautiful you. You're absolutely beautiful
you. Look at you. You're fantastic you. I love you. I love

the bones of you. I do. You think it's too quick don't you.
But you can't see yourself. You're just . . . I'm in love with
you, I'm not joking. I've seen some women, but you. Let's
get back to what you are, beautiful. Did you just smile
then or did someone turn the lights on? You are beautiful
you. You stand for beauty. You sit for it too. Look how
you sit you, like a glamour model that's how. You . . .
You're quiet though, but I love that in a girl, love that,
don't get me wrong. You're beauty you. Beauty itself.
Beauty is you. You're marvellous as well as being beautiful
too, you. Yes, too good for this place I'll tell you that.
What's a beautiful girl like you doing in a place like this,
or whatever they say, is that what they say, who cares,
who cares now, eh? You are a star, and you don't even
know it. A star before you start. Everything about you's,
just . . . You are it. The beauty of all times. You're just
beautiful and that's it! Done, finished, it. Because you are
the most beautiful thing ever brought to this earth. And
you're for me you. You are for me. There's no bones about
it, none! Here's the back of my hand, here, here. And
here's the pen, number, number please, number, before I
stop breathing.

Maudie *has entered and taps him on the shoulder.*

Maudie Hiyah Moth.

Moth What are you doing here?

Maudie I'm your bleeding bird aren't I?

Moth (*looking round*) Yes, yes, but . . .

Maudie Moth. Moth she wasn't interested.

Moth How do you know that?

Maudie Believe me I know. Moth, Moth do you still love
me?

Moth Of course I do, get them in.

Maudie No, I'm not this time.

Moth Eh?

Maudie I've had a good talking to by some of the girls at work today. And they've told me once and for all. I've not to let you keep using me.

Moth Using. Using. You sing and I'll dance. Ha! No Maudie you know that's not me. But when I'm broke what can I do, I depend on those that say they love me to care for me. And anyway it's always been our way.

Maudie Stop. Stop now. Don't keep turning me over with your tongue.

Moth Maudie, my Maudie.

He takes her in his arms, kisses her. She swoons.

Maudie Oh here get the drinks in.

Moth (*he opens handbag*) Ah that sweet click. (*Takes out some money.*) Here I go.

He sets off around the other side of bar to get served.

Maudie Oh no. No. Look he's off with my money again . . . I said this wouldn't happen again and here it is, happened. I've got to get me some strength. Where is it? (*Makes a fist and twists it.*) Ah there. Hold that Maudie. Maudie, Maudie hold that.

Moth *on his way back with the drinks. Bumps into someone. Dolly bird.*

Moth Oops sorry love. Bumpsadaisy. You all right . . .

Maudie Moth!

Moth See you. Better get these over to me sister. (*Passing others.*) 'Scuse me. (*Others.*) Yep yep. (*Others.*) Beep beep. Here we go Maud.

Maudie What were you . . . (*Shows fist to* **Moth**.)

Moth (*giving drink*) And here's your speciality.

Maudie Aww you always get it just right. Nobody gets it like you. The ice, the umbrella.

Moth Of course. Of course.

Maudie *kisses him.*

Maudie Oh look, I'm going again. All over you.

Moth That's all right, just watch the shirt.

They drink. He begins looking around. She looks at him looking around. She makes the fist again.

Maudie Look at me will you. Look at your eyes, they're everywhere, up every skirt, along every leg, round every bra rim. Why oh why do you keep chasing women!

Moth Oh we're not going to have to go through all this again are we petal. Is this the girls at work priming you?

Maudie Yes a bit, no a bit. I don't know. I can't remember now, so much has been said. I just want you to stop it.

Moth But you know I can't stop myself.

Maudie But you never even get off with them.

Moth I know.

Maudie It's like the girls say, I hold all the cards.

Moth How do you mean?

Maudie I'm the only woman on earth interested in you.

Moth Well yes, but . . .

Maudie Moth let it all go and let's get settled down.

Moth I can't it's something I've always done and I guess I always will. (*Again looking at some women.*)

Maudie No, Moth, no . . . Oh how can I get it through to you.

Moth (*draining his glass empty*) Drink by drink.

Maudie No way. Buzz off Moth.

Moth Come on love, get them in. Let's have a few and forget all this. You pay, I'll order.

Maudie No.

Moth But Maudie, my Maudie.

Maudie No, I'm stopping the tap. I shall not be used.

Moth Used. Used. Well if that's how you feel I can always go you know.

He walks down the bar a bit, stops, looks back, walks down the bar a bit, stops, looks back. Falls over a stool. Picks it up, laughs to cover embarrassment, limps back to her.

Maudie, I've been thinking, all what you're saying's so true and right as always. I'm losing everything, my flair, my waistline, what's next to go – you? Will it be you next?

Maudie (*unmoved*) You'll try anything won't you, just to get into my handbag. The romantic approach, the comic approach, the concern for me approach, the sympathy approach. Does it never end?

Moth You forgot sexy in there.

She swings for him, he ducks.

No Maudie. You're right again. What does a princess like you see in a loser like me?

Maudie I don't know. Well I do. You're romantic, like something on the fade. I love that.

Moth (*moving in*) Oh Maudie, my Maudie.

As he does, she starts to melt again, he starts to reach into her handbag, she suddenly sees this and slams it shut on his hand.

Maudie Stop!

Moth Aw Maud. How can I prove I'm genuine to you? Here take everything on me, everything, everything. (*Starts* *frantically emptying his pockets*.) My last 10p, I'm going to give it to you!

Maudie I don't want your poxy ten.

Moth You say that now, you say that now Maud, but you don't know what it's going to turn into. I'm going to give you all I've got left. My final, last and only possession. (*Spins and drops it in Juke box*.) My dancing talent.

'Kiss' by Tom Jones comes on. **Moth** *dances.*

Moth 'Cause Maud, whatever you say. Whatever's said and done. I'm still a top dancer 'ant I hey?

Maudie Well you can move.

Moth I can Maud. I sure as hell can Maud. (*Dancing*.) I'm dancing for you Maudie. For you only. (*Dancing*.) Come on get up here with me.

She comes to him, puts her handbag on the floor, they dance.

Moth Who's lost it all now eh?

He really grooves it.

Maudie (*worried, embarrassed*) Moth.

Moth Come on doll.

Maudie Moth take it easy.

Moth Come on. Swing it. Let your back bone slip. Yeah let your . . . Awwwwwwwa Ow ow!!! (*Stops. Can't move*.)

Maudie Moth, oh God, what is it?

Moth Me back, me back. Help oh help.

Maudie What can I do! What can I do!

Moth Get me a chair, get me a gin.

Maudie (*feeling up his back*) Where is it? Where is it?

Moth There between the whiskey and the vodka.

Maudie Ooo another trick, you snide, you emperor of snide! (*Hits him.*)

Moth No, no Maud. Really, you've got it all wrong. It's real. Arwwwwww. Get me to a chair!

Maudie It's real is it you swine?

Moth Real. Real.

Maudie Real is it?

Moth (*nodding*) Arrgh. Arrgh.

Maudie Okay let's test it.

Moth How?

She takes out a fiver and holds it in front of him. He tries to go for it, but he can't.

Maudie (*amazed*) It is true. (*Starts circling him.*) Trapped. At last after all these years, I finally have that fluttering Moth pinned down. Ha.

Moth Oh Maudie what you gonna do?

Maudie Let's see. Let's see here.

Moth Don't muck about now. I'm dying here, arrrgh, dying.

Maudie So if, if, I help, what do I get out of it?

Moth Anything! Anything!

Maudie Anything, anything eh?

Moth Yes, yes, arrrrgh.

Maudie Okay, make an honest woman of me now.

Moth No, never, arrrr.

Maudie Okay, see you love.

Moth No. Don't go Maud please.

Maudie Sorry love, have to, love to stay but . . . 'bye. And if any of you try to help him, you'll have me to deal with, and my handbag.

Maudie *blows him a kiss as she goes. Exits.*

Moth MAUD! Will you marry me?

Maudie (*coming back*) Sorry?

Moth Will you marry me?

Maudie YES! OH YESSSSSSSSS! (*She comes running to him and hugs him.*)

Moth (*she's hurt his back*) AARRRRGHHHH!

Maudie Oh sorry love.

Still in embrace she guides him to a stool.

Moth A a aa a.

She props him against stool and bar, he is stiff like a board.

Moth Ah.

Maudie Oh Oh. (*Cuddling him.*) Oh. (*Suddenly serious.*) Do you still mean it?

Moth I mean it. I mean it. Singleness is all over for me.

Maudie (*hugging him again as best she can*) Oh Moth you won't regret this.

Moth Arrgh. I know. I know.

Maudie I'll get us a taxi. Hold on now. Be brave. You poor thing.

She rushes out.

Moth (*turns, as best he can, to girl at front*) You're beautiful you. Look at you. You're fantastic you.

Blackout.

Landlady *enters from where they exited.*

Landlady (*calling back*) Handcuff him Maudie, handcuff him now. (*To audience.*) Look at that Maudie, over the moon and back, she wants to watch herself with that scallywag. Ahh, I enjoy a lull like this, you can get a decent chat in can't you? He hates lulls, if the till's not singing he starts crying. (*Waves to someone.*) All right. (*To someone else.*) Hiyah, I'll try and get over there in a minute. I like that part of pub life, the people. That's why it's a peach in here, so many people pairing up in front of your very eyes, very heart-warming, heart-rending. (*Looks off.*) Look at Pigoh go, the prat. (*Shouts.*) Hey you all right with those crates?

Landlord (*shouts from off*) Course I am. Bugger off!

Big crash is heard.

Landlady *titters.*

Landlord (*off*) OH MY GOD! MY PROFITS!

Landlady I don't know. Without me this place would collapse around the bastard, it really would. I'm the brains behind the operation you might say. He's got no idea really, he knows how to run around, but not how to run a pub. Sad but true, but funny too. You've got to laugh haven't you? This is our life, this public house and all who 'ale' in her. No social life, family life. Work, business, pleasure, all pulled from behind the bar, and beyond that only a loveless bed to lie in. Still, I have my consolations, like sipping away Pigoh's profits, and really, well there's never a dull moment when you deal in liquor. And you get to meet the choicest of people. Like this old love here.

Old Man *enters*.

Landlady How do Pops.

Old Man How do love.

Landlady What you on, a bitter or a stout?

Old Man Mild please.

Landlady Nothing like a change.

Old Man That's right dear.

Landlady You're a lovely old bugger you. Why don't you and me run away together. Just whisk me off me feet, I wouldn't say no.

Old Man Ha Ha.

Landlady Oh well, there you go Pops. (*Gives him drink.*) No, have it on me.

Old Man (*trying to pay*) Nay, here.

Landlady No, my treat.

Old Man Thank you.

Landlady My pleasure. (*Off to serve someone else.*) Yes love. (*Exits.*)

Old Man Howdo. (*Sups beer.*)

Pause.

They all think I'm quiet. (*Sups.*)

Long pause.

But there's a good reason for that.

Pause.

I'm having a very good time within.

Pause.

(*Smiles.*) With my wife. She's dead, but still with me. Not like a ghost or any of that old kak.

Pause.

It's just a feeling. (*Sups.*)

Don't go yet, I'm not mad tha' knows.

Pause.

Sometimes if the feeling's not come of its own
I can generally bring it on
by touching our teapot,
brown pot,
and this'll start something
brewing,
sweet,
present,
soft
as her cotton hair.

Long pause.

Then it deepens. (*Closes his eyes.*)

Pause.

She's here now.

Nice.

She was here when I came in
but it's more better now.

Pause.

It's like . . .

Pause.

Being held.

It's just

comfort of her
without anything else.

Pause.

She's gone now. (*Opens eyes.*) So that's how we come and go to each other during the day. (*Sups.*)

Pause.

And how deep we do soak in each other sometimes. So deep I can hardly stand from the chair. And this is how I think I'll go one day. I'll just tag on and slip off with her when she leaves. And somebody will come round to our house and find my empty shell. (*Chuckles, drinks, rests.*) Life's just passing in and out in't it? Very comfortable, very nice to know that. (*Finishes drink.*) Ta tar. (*Goes.*)

Landlady *enters with sandwich.*

Landlady Cheese and onion! (*To someone close by.*) Keep your eyes off, you. I've done this as a favour for . . . Where is she? (*Sees her, goes to her.*) There you are love, get that down you. (*Takes money.*) Tar. (*To someone else.*) Love the trousers, who'd have thought they'd come back in. Only joking love, very natty them.

Landlord *enters.*

Landlord The queen of tittle tattle.

Landlady Sod off.

Landlord Out of the cellar and into the boxing ring, that's me. (*Hits the bar side, enters bar.*)

Landlady (*also enters bar, puts money in till*) Ting ting, tills away, round bleedin' one.

Landlord Will you back off for once.

Landlady Never.

Landlord (*to customer*) Same again Jack? (*Puts glass up to optics.*)

Landlady (*to her customer*) Just the one pet, sure. (*She reaches up to optics, their arms cross.*)

Landlord What's up with you tonight?

Landlady I think you know.

Landlord (*gives drink, takes money*) Ta mate.

Landlady (*gives drink, takes money*) Thanks love.

They both come back to till and put money in.

Landlord I don't know what you're on about.

Landlady (*she closes till*) Ting ting, round two. Yes you do, yes you do.

Landlord Run a pub.

Landlady (*turns into corner to work*) That's it, turn to the ropes when the jabs get too close.

Landlord (*looks up*) What the bloody hell's this coming in!

Landlady Ting ting, match postponed!

Landlord It's a stag party. Man the pumps, pull out the stops, raise the prices, come on let's polish them off. You take the spirits, I'll take the beers.

Landlady *leaves without him noticing.*

Well then Gents, what's it to be? (*He listens to the orders of the imaginary crowd, nodding as he does so. Then he repeats the orders back to them, at rapid speed.*) Five pints of lager, three bitter, two whiskeys one with ice, one without, gin, gin, gin and tonic. Treble tequila, Guinness, spritzer, brown and bitter, Barbican, Budweiser, Bloody Mary, Black Velvet and a Becks, Triple X, Tiopepe, Martini, vodka and shandy and a brandy, Pernod, peanuts, crisps, crisps, crisps, crisps, crisps, crisps, crisps, two rum and okey cokey colas, and a Cherry B and cider for the groom. We'll sort that for you lads, won't we dear, (*Turns to see she's gone.*) dear, *dear!* (*Hits the bar, exits.*)

Lights up on **Mrs Iger**, *arms folded, perched on bar stool nodding to the long scream and the opening strains of Led Zeppelin's 'Whole Lotta Love'. Music suddenly stops. She speaks.*

Mrs Iger I love big men. Big quiet strong men. That's all I want. I love to tend to them. I like to have grace and flurry round them. I like their temple arms and pillar legs and synagogue chests and big mouth and teeth and tongue like an elephant's ear. And big carved faces like a naturreal cliff side, and the Roman empire bone work. And you can really dig deep into 'em, can't you? And there's so much. Gargantuan man, like a Roman Empire, with a voice he hardly uses, but when he does it's all rumbling under his breast plate. So big, big hands, big everything. Like sleeping by a mountain side. Carved men. It's a thrill if you see them run, say for a bus, pounding up the pavement. Good big man, thick blood through tubular veins, squirting and washing him out. It must be like a bloody big red cavernous car wash in there, in him, and all his organs and bits hanging from the rib roof, getting a good daily drenching in this good red blood. They are so bloody big you think they'll never die, and that's another reason you want them. Bloody ox men, Hercules, Thor, Chuck Connors, come on, bring your heads down and take from my 'ickle hand. Let me groom and coddle you. And herd you. Yes, let me gather all ye big men of our Isles and herd you up and lead you across America. You myth men. Myth men. Myth men. Big men love ya.

Little man approaches her.

Mr Iger Dear, I'm having difficulty getting to the bar again. Would you go?

Mrs Iger No. You get back in there and bring us drinks. Now.

Mr Iger I'll have another try shall I dear?

Mrs Iger No, not a try. Get them here. It's pathetic.

Mr Iger (*trying to get through the crowd*) 'Scuse . . . sorry . . .

Ow . . . Are you in the queue . . . Oh . . . Sorry . . . Could
I squeeze . . . ? No . . . Thanks . . . (*Suddenly wiping himself.*)
It's all right. It's all right. My fault . . . Whose turn is it,
do you know? . . . Well I only asked . . . (*Manages to squeeze
in to bar.*) Two please . . . Hello . . . two . . . could I . . .
'scuse . . . Here love! Ah yes, yes, could I . . . What? (*Leans
back and looks up.*) Oh yes I think you, perhaps, were first,
that's right. Please go ahead . . . Oh no, she's going to kill
me. We've been in here an hour and we've not drank yet.
It's always the same. Dear, deary me.

He suddenly notices two unattended drinks by him.

What about these two here. I couldn't. (*Looks about.*)
Could I?((*Looks about.*) I have to.

He slips off with them and back to her.

Mr Iger Here we go dear.

Mrs Iger At last. (*She takes a drink then splutters out.*) What's
this, we don't have alcoholic drinks.

Mr Iger I know, but that's all they had.

Mrs Iger You. Oh well, I'm not waiting another hour,
they'll have to do. But I must say, I must say, it is another
typical cock up by Mr Feeble man. I mean what's to
getting to a bar for a drink? Are you man or mouse?

He tries to speak.

Squeak, squeak, there's my answer. You should do
something about all this. I mean it's typical, too typical of
the little. I mean if you were big, big as I wanted, well,
well . . .

Mr Iger *suddenly cracks.*

Mr Iger (*crazed*) Right then drinks is it? Drinks. I can get
drinks. Right then. Here I go. I'm coming through. (*Barges
through to the bar.*) Straight through. I get them in, me.
Drinks. I'm the drink man. I was before everyone, me.

Everyone. (*To someone.*) Shut your face fatso. Come on now drinks, drinks, drinks for me, us, short ones, long ones . . .

As he continues raving, **Mrs Iger** *comes through.*

Mrs Iger Excuse me. Let me through. Thank you.

Mr Iger . . . I'll take all them orange ones, them green and them brown. Come on drinks here, come on, come on drinks . . .

She hits him on the back of the head, he stops.

Mrs Iger Now what's to do?

Mr Iger Drinks you wanted. I was before everyone. Drinks I say.

Mrs Iger Calm.

Mr Iger I can get drinks. I can. Oh yes.

Mrs Iger Calm.

Mr Iger Drinks I will get, will.

Mrs Iger Calm.

Mr Iger Drinks.

Mrs Iger Calm.

He goes quiet.

Mrs Iger What is it?

He's quiet.

It's me, isn't it with just too much talk of the large.

He nods.

Ay dear, what have I done to you, my dinky.

Putting her arm around him.

Mr Iger Dinky?

Mrs Iger Yes. Come here my detailed little man.

She takes him in her arms.

Your weediness is welcome here.

They separate.

Come away now. Come on. My compact chap. (*Briskly.*)
We'll do something nice, take a walk, get some fresh air.

They exit. Offstage.

Mr Iger Dear?

Mrs Iger Yes?

Mr Iger Does this mean I can sleep in the bed tonight?

Mrs Iger Don't push it.

Landlord *enters holding a bottle high.*

Landlord Here it is. Last one ever. I knew I'd seen one in
the cellar. A bloody 'Bull's eye' brown. Look at that then.
(*He undoes it.*) There you go. (*Gives it to customer.*)

Landlady *comes in, begins serving someone as soon as she enters.*

Landlady Whiskey love? Yep. (*She turns to get it.*)

Landlord (*to* **Landlady**) Hey, look who's here having a
bloody 'Bull's eye' brown.

Landlady Smelly Jimmy. Well well. We've not seen you
for years.

She continues her job of filling glass with whiskey.

How are you?

Landlord
Landlady } (*in response*) Oh we're all right.

Landlady Well I am.

She turns to serve her customer. Then, in response to something Jimmy says:

Eh. (*She drops glass, it breaks. She can't speak.*) Don't you know?

Landlord (*quickly*) Hey Jimeny, come round here mate. This side here. Come on. (*Leads him off.*) You'll remember these lot of ugly mugs won't you? (*Offstage.*) Hey, look what the cat's brought in.

Landlady (*to her customer*) Sorry love.

Gets another whiskey for them. Takes money.

Tar. Tar.

Puts it in till.

Landlady *starts kicking glass under bar.*

Landlord *enters.*

Landlord Don't do that.

He gets down picking glass up.

Landlady Why? I thought you liked things shoved out of sight.

Landlord Don't know what you mean.

Landlady You do.

Landlord *turns away, starts doing something.*

Landlady Don't you think it's funny someone should say that, tonight of all nights. Don't you?

Landlord (*picking up empty bottle off bar*) Imagine finding a bloody 'Bull's eye' brown, eh?

Landlady Don't you?

Landlord I'll save that empty as a memento.

He puts it on shelf. She grabs it and shoves it in bin.

Landlady There's already two empty mementos behind this bar.

Landlord (*turning to serve someone*) Two pints sir. One lager, one bitter.

Landlady (*behind him, penetratingly*) Don't you think it funny though someone should ask . . . Don't you?

Landlord (*puts glass under lager tap*) Lager.

Landlady Don't you? Don't you?

Landlord (*worn down, puts glass under bitter tap*) Sorry, bitter's off. I'll just go and see to that. (*Goes quickly.*)

Landlady *lifts glass of lager, gives to customer. Tries bitter tap. Laughs.*

Landlady He was wrong again. I thought as much. Look at that. Bitter's never off here dear. (*Filling glass. Looking after* **Landlord**.) Never.

Interval – if required.

Landlord *enters collecting glasses.*

Landlord Busy now, eh? You can see it busy now, eh? The hectic hour. There's been a lot of copping offs round that side, two fallings out here, and a fight, three proposals of marriage round there, and a birth in the snug. And it's nowhere near last orders yet! Not really. Not really. I always say that about this time. I like a crack with the customers now and again. Better than a crack from them, eh? Eh? So you're still here then. Glad to see it. Keep drinking that's my motto, don't stop till you drop, that's my other. Glass harvesting time now. Collect 'em in.

Collect 'em in, wish they'd bring their own. Come on, sip, swig, and sup (*Under breath.*) ya buggers. That's right. All right if I take your glasses love. Not the ones you're wearing. No put them back. (*Turns to audience.*) Bloody hell.

Landlord *crosses to woman,* **Lesley,** *sitting on her own.*

Landlord Hello love, where is he tonight then?

Lesley *mumbles something.*

Landlord Hey?

Lesley *mumbles again.*

Landlord At bar?

Lesley Yeah.

Landlord (*looks round*) Looks like you've lost him then. You'll never find him again in all that lot. Look at 'em all. Lovely thirsty boozers. My favourites. Better get her back and serving. (*Looks off.*) Look at her entertaining the rabble.

Landlord *goes.*

Lesley *looks around, then looks down. Looks around, then looks down.*

Roy *comes over with drinks.*

Roy What were he on about?

Lesley Nowt, he were just collecting glasses.

Roy Oh. Here you are. (*Puts drinks down. Sits.*) She's a character that landlady.

Lesley She is.

They drink. Pause.

Lesley What you on?

Roy Mild.

She nods. They sit in silence.

Roy There's more strange things happen in a pub than there do on T.V. Eh?

Lesley Aye. Could I just . . . ?

Roy Bloody hell, what did your last slave die of? Bloody Hell! I've only just sat down.

Lesley No. I wanted to know if I could go to loo.

Roy 'Course you can. Okay go.

She stands up.

But don't be long.

She begins to move.

Hey, and look down.

Lesley Eh?

Roy Keep your eyes down. Every time you look up, you look at men you.

Lesley I don't.

Roy (*pointing at her*) Eh, hey, no back chat. (*Looks quickly around, making sure no one's heard him.*) Go on.

She goes.

Roy (*to someone*) Mike.

Pause.

(*To someone else.*) Sandy.

Pause.

She comes back and sits.

Roy What did you have?

Lesley Eh?

Roy What did you have, one or two?

Lesley One.

Roy You were a long time for a one.

Lesley There was someone in as well.

Roy Christ, I s'pose you got chatting.

Lesley No.

Roy No.

Lesley No.

Roy Don't 'no' me.

She edges back.

Did you say 'owt about me?

Lesley No.

Roy Who did you talk about then, someone else?

Lesley No.

Roy I told you with your no's. Who did you talk about?

Lesley We didn't even talk.

Roy Didn't even talk. Don't gi' me that. Two women in a woman's shithouse and they don't speak. You must think I'm soft. Do you?

Lesley What?

Roy Think I'm soft.

Lesley I don't know.

Roy What do you mean, don't know?

Lesley Well, I can't say no you said.

Roy Oh, if I said put your hand in the fire would you? Would you?

She shakes her head.

Roy Why not?

She looks away.

Roy No but you can talk about men in women's toilets can't you love, eh?

She keeps looking away.

If you don't answer, that means yes.

Lesley No.

Roy If you say no, two things happen: one I know you're lying, two I think about hittin' you in the face.

Lesley *looks down. He nods to someone across bar.*

Roy So, do you wanna stay here or move on?

Lesley Mmm.

Roy Christ I don't know why I bother. You've no conversation have you? Have you?

Lesley Mmm.

Roy See what I'm on about. I might as well go out with a piece of shit from that favourite woman's bog of yours, where you spent all our night.

Pause.

Do you want some more crisps?

Lesley Mmm.

Roy Well liven up then and you might get some later on. What about some 'Wotsits'?

Lesley Yes.

Roy Well there you are then. Liven up and you might get some 'Wotsits'.

Pause.

Roy They've done a nice job in here 'ant they, eh? He did a lot of it himself, knocked the snug out and everything. What's over there?

Lesley Eh?

Roy What's over there so interesting?

Lesley Nothing, I just moved me head I . . .

Roy I see. Watching the darts were you? Eh?

Lesley No I . . .

Roy What?

Lesley I don't know.

Roy Don't know. I do. See that little git in the jeans and shirt, there, him.

She looks.

Roy Okay you've seen enough now. Well I could break him like that, with my knee and my arms. Break the little wanker like that. Okay? Okay?

Lesley Okay.

Roy Would you be sad?

Lesley I don't know. I don't even know him.

Roy But you'd like to wouldn't you?

Lesley No.

Roy No. Are you sure?

She nods her head.

Roy It's just that 'okay' sounded a bit sad.

Lesley What 'okay'?

Roy That 'okay' you said before sounded a bit sad. After I'd said I'd break the little wanker. That one.

Lesley (*confused*) Oh.

Roy *stares at her a long time.*

Roy Don't make me feel small.

Lesley I'm not.

Roy I'm not having you or him or anyone making me feel small.

Lesley I'm not.

Roy Well, I just said all that then, and then felt small.

Lesley What?

Roy About him and you, and that 'okay', and you made me feel small after. When it was your fault, I said it in the first place, for looking at him.

Lesley (*beaten*) Oh.

Roy Well.

Lesley What?

Roy Are you not going to say sorry?

Lesley Sorry.

Roy Right. (*To someone across bar, raises his glass.*) Aye get 'em down yeah. Ha.

Silence.

Roy You've gone quiet. What you thinking of?

Lesley Nothing.

Roy No, no. Hold on. No. Who you thinking of?

Lesley (*pleading*) Oh Roy.

Roy No, no. When someone's quiet they're thinking, right?

Lesley Maybe.

Roy Maybe. That's a funny word to say, maybe. What you saying maybe for? That means you were. Who?

Lesley I wasn't.

Roy Who? If you wasn't, you would have said no. Who were you thinking of?

Lesley No one.

Roy Who? (*Waits.*) Who?

She shakes her head.

Roy Hey, remember what I said about no. Who?

She looks down.

Who?

She looks down more.

Who?

Lesley (*suddenly jumps up*) No one. No one at all. Can't I even have me own mind!

Roy (*embarrassed*) Sit down. Sit down.

Lesley I can't win. If I said I was thinking of every man in here naked, or I said I was thinking of you and the baby, it wouldn't make any difference. You'd still find a way of torturing me wouldn't you? Torturing! Torturing!

She storms out.

He looks round grinning, embarrassed.

Pause.

She comes back in.

Lesley I need the front door key.

Roy (*gently*) Hey, sit down love. Please sit.

She still stands.

I'm sorry. I realise what I must have done to you now. I don't know what it is. It's 'cause I care like. You know. I get carried away. Come on, sit down, please.

She does.

(*Soft.*) I didn't expect you to do that love.

Suddenly slaps her.

(*Vicious.*) You'll never do it again.

Instant blackout.

Landlord *going behind bar.*

Landlord Winding down now, winding down. We're over the top of the hill and half way down the other side. In other words the mad rush is over. So . . . (*Reaches for a glass, puts it under optics.*) Should I? Shouldn't I? Should I? Shouldn't I? Or . . . (*Puts glass under pumps.*) Should I? Shouldn't I? Should I? Or . . .

Landlady *walks in and goes straight to optics, puts her glass under. Lets measure one, two, three come out. He is watching agape. She goes and lounges against bar.*

Landlord What's going on?

Landlady Where?

Landlord Here. With your (*Mimics action.*) one, two, three. We don't do all this for nothing you know.

Landlady Ah, sod off.

Landlord How many have you had tonight anyway?

Landlady Three dray men, five regulars, a few lager louts, and the 'Cheesies' rep.

Landlord It wouldn't surprise me. It would not surprise me.

She lifts her glass in a cheers.

Landlord Come on how much? Let me smell your breath. Let me.

He goes up to her face, she turns away, he sniffs.

Landlady Don't get too close, we might accidentally kiss.

Landlord You're half sozzled, aren't you?

Landlady I'd say more than half actually.

Landlord Bloody great in'it. Bloody great.

Landlady Oh shut up.

He suddenly grabs glass off her and throws its contents down the sink. She's angry at first. Then just lounges back. Laughs.

Landlord I'd rather do that, than you have it.

Landlady Oh.

Landlord (*still looking down sink*) Yes, I would.

Landlady Oh I bet it hurt that, like throwing your blood away.

Landlord You just don't care any more do you? It may have escaped your notice, but we're trying to make a living here.

Landlady (*picking up a glass again*) This helps me to keep living here.

She goes toward optics with it. He puts his hand on hers to stop her.

Landlady Get off.

Landlord No.

Landlady Get off or I'll scream like I've been stabbed.

Landlord Do it then.

She begins to open her mouth. He lets her go. She goes to optic, gets another drink.

Landlord I'm going, I can't watch this.

Landlady What, me drinking, or your precious profits on the drip?

Landlord *doesn't look at her. He just leaves.*

She goes to drink. But can't now. Puts it down. Puts her hand over her eyes.

Blackout.

Lights up.

Fred *enters and sits.* **Alice** *enters, eating crisps, turns T.V. on, sits beside him.*

Fred Well, shall we get a drink in?

Alice I wouldn't mind so much.

Fred Well, get them in then.

Alice I will after this next programme.

Fred Okay.

Silence. She starts looking round.

Fred What you doing?

Alice I'm just looking round.

Fred You're doing counting things again.

Alice I'm not.

Fred You damn are. Do you want to go back in that white place wid' the closed doors?

Alice No fear, no.

Fred Well hang onto yourself then.

Alice I've never been the same since Elvis died.

Fred You killed him.

Alice How?

Fred By buying his records which gave him money for drugs which killed him.

Alice The King never took drugs.

Fred Not freaky drugs but slimming pills and all that, dried his blood up, constipated him. Choked his bum, he died of a choked bum.

Alice Such kingliness gone.

Fred You're fat and old.

Alice You're exactly the same.

She looks at the T.V.

Alice He's exactly the same as well.

Fred Who?

Alice Him there, behind Kirk Douglas. Very Fat.

Fred He is too. He's not going to get on that palomino horse is he?

Alice No way.

Fred He bloody is you know. You just watch.

They watch.

Alice No, they've both gone out the picture now.

Fred Do you think that's it with them now?

Alice Probably.

Fred I hope the horse comes back towards the end.

Alice It won't.

Fred What a swizz.

Silence.

Fred If I was at home I'd turn the bloody thing off.

Alice I know you would, that's why we came to the pub.

Fred Well it's not to drink that's for sure. I've only had two.

Alice Well you'll have to hang on till we're both ready.

Fred I'm ready now.

Alice Well I nearly am.

Silence.

Fred Well, what we waiting for, the film or the crisps?

Alice All the lot.

She finishes crisps: tips the packet and drains it. While he's not looking, she blows it up and pops it in his ear. They look round and start laughing.

Fred Oh ha, I don't know.

Alice Hee hee.

Fred Ha.

Suddenly points at television screen.

Fred There's the palomino again. Look at him go!

Alice I don't believe it, and the fat man too. They've gone now.

Fred I recognised him then. He was in the background in some other film we watched.

Alice I wonder if we'll see him in something else.

Fred Let's remember him, we'll give him a name.

Alice What?

Fred 'Fat-Fat'.

Alice 'Fat-Fat' what?

Fred 'Fat-Fat Palomino'.

Alice 'Fat-Fat Palomino' our favourite star.

Fred He's probably dead now, these are old pictures.

Alice Aw, I hope not.

Fred Oh, don't have the water works.

Alice I'm not. I'm not that sad about him.

Fred He was a bloody good extra though.

Alice He was.

Fred I wouldn't mind trying that.

Alice You're too fat and old.

Fred He was fat and old.

Alice Yeah, but he was a different fat and old.

Fred What do you mean?

Alice He was American-Ranch-style fat and old.

Fred What's that mean?

Alice There's different fat and olds all over the world.

Fred And what fat and old am I? English fat and old?

Alice No, sad fat, poor old.

Fred Well now I know. Anyway, you're just fat and old. Fat and old all over your little chair.

Alice We're middle-aged anyway.

Fred I know, but we look old with our fat.

They both watch tele awhile. The film ends.

Fred It's finished. Turn the tele off.

Alice Why?

Fred We turned it on.

Alice You do it.

Fred I can't with my legs.

She does. She comes back and sits.

Alice (*sings*) Are you lonesome tonight?

Fred So get them in now.

Alice (*sings*) Do you miss me tonight?

Fred Shall we get them in now?

Alice (*sings*) Are you sorry we drifted apart? (*Goes silent.*)

Fred You've gone again haven't you?

Alice It's me nerves, I can't help it.

Fred Come on, let's go home and play records.

Alice I'll cry.

Fred I'll dabble your tears.

Alice We're close in our way.

Fred Close as we can get with our fat.

Alice We've been unlucky in life but luckyish in love.

Fred Yes.

Alice Will you call me Priscilla tonight?

Fred Yes I will. (*Pause.*) Will you call me 'Fat-Fat Palomino'?

They leave. Blackout.

Landlord *enters.*

LAST ORDERS NOW. COME ON. COME ON. LAST ORDERS. LAST. LADIES AND GENTS.

Begins collecting glasses.

(*To someone in audience.*) He's had a few too many an't he love? Look at that, eh. You wanna get him home. Do you know the fireman's lift?

Last orders everybody. We've reached the point of no
return. Last orders now. Come on slow throats. Last
orders at the bar.

(*To someone leaving.*) Goodnight. Take care now.

(*To someone as he collects lots of glasses up.*) Did you drink all
them yourself Missus? Bloody hell, you can come again
you can.

He stacks them on the bar.

Any more for any more?

Last orders.

Exits.

A **Woman** *enters, slightly drunk.*

Woman (*to audience*) Are they still serving? I mustn't leave
this corner for the moment. I'm the 'Other Woman', come
where she shouldn't to look at my man. My man and his
wife. I've not come incognito either. I've come as my
bloody self; drinky, smart, a little crumpled, used to being
dressed up at the wrong time in the wrong places. In the
only car on a car park after dark. In strange houses in the
afternoon. At bus stops in last night's make-up. And I'm
not having it no, no more Mister. (*She takes out a fag,
fumbles with it, drops it.*) I've come here tonight, so he can
see us both. Not one in one world and one in another, but
both under the same light and choose. (*As in a child's
choosing rhyme.*) Ip, dip, ip, dip, ip, dip. You see this is the
last time I'm going to love. I haven't got it in me to go
again. So it's to be him, or it's to be something else, but
not another man. No, no more. Where's that fagarette?
Did I drop it? Toots to it, toots to the lot of it. Did he look
then? (*She tugs at her scarf, it falls.*) He did, I'm sure. Oh
Jesu! Jesu! I want him. I want to wave and scream. She

doesn't know, you know. I can tell, see, see that laugh she makes, too free, too free by far. I think. That's how it is in flick and shadow land, it's all thinking of others and their movements and I am sick to the soul with it. What will he do? What will she say? Will he come? Will he cancel? Is that the door? Was that the car? Dare I shower? Will he ring? Most times these wives, you know, they don't even want them. They won't have love with them, you know. They put them down, you know. But they won't let them loose. My God, they will not let them loosey. And I love loosey. Oh my God, he's coming over. Face him, face him. No shift, shift, shift. Face him. Shift. (*She turns away.*)

Out of the dark the **Landlord** *approaches, collecting glasses. She turns, they come face to face. Pause.*

Where is he?

Landlord Who, love?

Woman A man and his woman, they were coming this way.

Landlord They just passed you love, and went out.

Woman Follow that couple.

She rushes after them.

Landlady (*from offstage*) Watch out love, you nearly had me over.

Landlady Who was that?

Landlord She left her scarf.

Landlady Well, take it after her quick unless you want to wear it.

Landlord *takes it and exits.*

Landlady *starts to put a few bottles, glasses away.*

Landlady (*to someone leaving*) Goodnight. Yeah, see you. You do if you dare. Tara. (*To someone else.*) One for the road is it? Okey doke. There you go love, thanks. (*To someone at door.*) Night.

She turns back and starts: a little boy is there.

Boy Is me Dad here?

Landlady What do you say lovey?

Boy Is me Dad here?

Landlady Well I don't know love, do you want to hitch up here and see if you can see him?

Boy *nods.* **Landlady** *lifts him up on counter.*

Landlady Can you see him?

Boy *shakes his head.*

Landlady What's his name?

Boy Frank.

Landlady Is it Frank Leigh?

Boy *nods.*

Landlady Oh, he's gone love, he left a while ago.

Boy *nods at her words, and then starts crying his eyes out.*

Landlady Oh dear, come on love, don't cry, eh?

Boy I want my Dad.

Landlady I know you do love. I know. Where've you been?

Boy (*in sobs*) He left me outside with some pop and some crisps and he's forgot me.

He starts crying again.

Landlady (*loving him*) Now, now, eh.

Boy I want my Dad.

Landlady Don't worry love, he'll be back. Listen now, listen. Is your Mummy at home?

Boy No, she's in hospital.

Landlady Well, I'll tell you what, if he doesn't turn up soon we'll go and find him, shall we? How's that, eh?

He seems to have calmed now. Then he suddenly starts crying again.

Landlady It's all right love. Hey, hey, come on now. I'll tell you what, let's have some more crisps shall we, while we're waiting eh?

He nods.

Landlady Okay. (*She goes behind bar.*) Let's see what we've got here. (*Suddenly she looks over and beyond him.*) Now look who I can see. Look who's just come back. (*Looking towards door.*)

Boy (*looks*) DAD! (*Tries to jump off, can't.*)

Landlady *helps him down, he almost starts to belt off.*

Landlady Hey, hey. You forgot something.

Gives him crisps. Then holds his face between her hands and kisses his forehead, lingering, looking at him, the child looking back. Then suddenly she comes round.

Go on now. Off you go.

He runs out towards his Dad. She watches him go. Then goes behind the bar. Gets a drink.

Landlord (*enters, calling back*) Hey Frank, what have I told you about kids in here? I don't know.

(*To customers.*) All right, could you drink up now. Tar. (*To* **Landlady**.) Drop the towel over the taps love.

She just turns away.

(*He takes another glass.*) Tar. (*Holds it up to look, turns it upside down, truly empty.*) You enjoyed that one didn't you. Bloody hell. Okay, see you. 'Night. Can we have your glasses please. Thank you. Tar. See you. Sleep tight.

Landlady 'Bye love.

Landlord Well that's that then. Another one over. Will you bolt up? What's up with you? Oh, I'll do it.

He goes off, hear bolts going.

He comes back in.

Landlord Come on then. (*He starts to get stuck in with the glasses.*)

Landlady Did you see that little boy?

Landlord Yeah I saw him. (*Still working.*)

Landlady Do you know what day it is today?

Landlord Yeah, another working one. Come on, let's get these lot away.

Landlady Okay. (*She puts her arm on top of counter and walks forward, all the glasses smashing to floor.*)

Landlord What you doing? OH CHRIST!

They stare at each other.

Landlady Shall I clear that side now?

She goes to do it. He grabs her.

Landlady Go on, hit me. But hit me hard.

Landlord *lets her go. He returns to work.*

Landlord I know what day it is.

Landlady Eh?

Landlord I said, I know what day it is. What do you think I am, stone?

He stops working. Looks down sink like he's going to be sick.

Landlady Seems that way.

Landlord *grabs a glass, goes to optic, lets two measures out.*

Landlady Don't.

Landlord Why not? You do.

Landlady I can stop. Oh go on, what's it to me.

Landlord That's more like it. That's nearer to it. I was getting a bit worried there, sounded like care. (*Drinks. Carries on working.*) Come on.

Landlady Eh?

Landlord Let's get going.

Landlady Is that it then? That's how you think it can go again. One little explosion, two little explosions, have a drink, carry on.

Landlord Huh. (*Working.*)

Landlady That's what's been going on for years and years. Every time we try to talk about it.

Landlord I don't know what you're on about.

Landlady You do.

Landlord Look, another time eh?

Landlady No. Not this night you don't. No slipping away. I want to talk about things.

Landlord Well I don't, okay?

Landlady You're a bastard. How the hell am I going to get this out then? How the hell am I going to get it out? I've no one to love it out of me, I've no one to knock it out of me. Just a blank man.

Landlord Tough.

She starts randomly knocking glasses off.

Landlord Don't hurt my pub!

She starts laughing.

Landlady It's not a person you know.

Landlord I know. But that's the sorry state of it. It's all I've got to care for.

Landlady Oh dear.

Landlord I hate you.

Landlady I hate you harder.

Landlord If that's the case, in these few precious hours we have to ourselves, why do we have to waste them on each other?

Landlady Because seven years ago tonight our son died . . .

There's a knock at the door. He goes out to it.

Landlord (*offstage*) No we're closed. No, no take away. No.

Bolts again. Comes back in. Continues clearing away.

Landlady I feel sick. That's the first time I've said that for almost as many years. Why did it sound corny on my lips? (*Looks up, he's not listening.*) You're not listening.

Landlord Well. (*Pause, cleaning.*) You've got to carry on. (*Pause, cleaning.*) You know that as well as I do.

She suddenly screams long, chilling and loud.

He turns to look at her, doesn't go to her, just watches until she's finished.

Then she looks up at him, like a shot animal.

Landlady I can't stand it no more! The blame hurts and burns too much.

Landlord I never blamed you.

Landlady Liar.

Landlord I did not blame you, all right?

Landlady Who did you blame then, yourself?

Landlord No.

Landlady Who did you blame then, him?

Landlord Don't say things like that!

Landlady What, leave him out of this, like he never existed, is that what you're saying?

Landlord Stop. Stop with your filth!

Landlady What? . . . You're mad.

Landlord (*back to work*) Leave the dead.

Landlady God you're worse than me.

Landlord (*working on*) I'm worse than no one, just leave it, eh?

Landlady Look we've got to get this out for our own sanity.

Landlord You worry about that, I'm all right.

Landlady It's rotted us.

Landlord Well, what's the point of bothering then?

Landlady You cold gone bastard.

Landlord Aye.

She grabs up a glass to him. He turns to her, lifts his chin.

Landlord Go on break it and shove it in where it's soft. Go on. (*Waits.*) You want to, and I don't mind.

She drops glass.

Landlady What have we come to?

She turns away.

He stays in that position, chin up.

Pause.

She turns back. She looks at him standing there like that.

Still in that position, like a statue, he speaks. Eyes closed.

Landlord I loved it when we all loved. When we all were loving. Him and . . . When we were . . . Me and you bickered like we do now, all very funny, all on the surface, but love was underneath then. Now it's hate. Hate for sure.

Silence.

Landlord *opens eyes.*

I see him every day.
My son.

Pause.

I remember when he could . . .
Pulling at the crates like his Dad.
He thought he could do it, didn't he?

I see him here like as . . .

In his pyjamas.

At night his hair was always . . . (*Touches his own head.*)
Peeping in the pub. You'd shout, but I'd always let him in, and lift him up and on the counter.

Oh God, how do you die when you're seven years old.

Covers his eyes.

Pause.

When it happened I had to turn away. I thought later I could turn back, but I couldn't. Nothing healed, it just went harder and harder and harder.

Landlady And you blamed.

Landlord No.

Landlady Liar!

Landlord No.

Landlady A blaming man. A stupid blaming man.

Landlord No.

Landlady Yes!

Landlord You were driving!

Landlady Yes!

Landlord Let's stop this.

Landlady You can't do that to me. It has to be out!

Landlord No more. (*Shakes his head.*)

Landlady Yes, all of it. We were flung. Cars in the back and side. And a over and a over. I looked at him, he was going like a rag doll, this way and that, this way and that, his little mouth wide open. Then I was gone. In the ambulance, bits I remember, some blanket round me, blood in the wool. At the hospital I remember nothing, just a black, red, black, red, like some old coal, coming and going for a very long time. When I came to I knew he'd gone. Later, one of the nurses told me. Later, you came. There were flowers everywhere. You told me you'd buried him, you said you couldn't keep his body all that time while I was in the coma. But I knew you'd done it because you blamed me.

Landlord No.

Landlady He went without my goodbye. I didn't see him in his suit and tie, in his little coffin. I saw him with his mouth wide open.

Landlord Stop.

Landlady No. No. I couldn't tell what was left between us in the hospital. But when I came home the cold set in. Really frightening cold. And we stood like strangers upstairs. And we've stood that way ever since.

He nods.

Pause.

Silence.

Landlord Please know now, I didn't blame you. And I didn't want to do that to you. But I couldn't touch anything. Please know. I had no blame. Just hard, everything hard.

Landlady Why couldn't you tell me that?

Landlord Couldn't say any . . . And from then on. All this time wouldn't talk about it, so you couldn't talk about it. I thought about it, but knew you thought I didn't. And in my quiet you thought I blamed, but I didn't. Such a lot of hurt inside. Solid. Hard.

Landlady We've held ourselves for all these years, sick of our own arms squeezing, squeezing.

They look at each other. It seems they're going to embrace. But he turns and takes a glass, and begins washing it.

Landlord In the morning, you bring his picture down and you put it up there, will you?

She nods.

They both start to clean up and put away a while, in silence.

Landlady I'll cash up tomorrow.

Landlord Aye. I'll just switch off.

He turns lights out.

In the dark.

Landlord I love you.

Landlady I love you too.

The Rise and Fall of
Little Voice

The Rise and Fall of Little Voice, produced by Michael Codron, was premièred in the Cottlesloe at the Royal National Theatre on 16 June 1992, with the following cast:

Mari Hoff	Alison Steadman
Little Voice (LV)	Jane Horrocks
Ray Say	Pete Postlethwaite
Sadie	Annette Badland
Billy	Adrian Hood
Phone Man	George Raistrick
Mr Boo	George Raistrick

Directed by Sam Mendes
Designed by William Dudley
Lighting by Mick Hughes
Music Terry Davies
Director of Movement Jane Gibson
Musicians Terry Davies (keyboards),
Michael Gregory (drums)

Stage Manager David Milling
Deputy Stage Manager Helen Bower
Assistant Stage Managers Andrew Eastcott
Liz Ryder

Place: A Northern Town

Time: now

Set: A living room, kitchen attached, open plan. Up left, stairs to LV's bedroom. At side an alley and lamp-post are visible.

Act One

Darkness.

Darkness.

A long scream from **Mari**.

Mari There's one.

She screams again.

Mari There's another one. You scream.

LV No.

Mari No, you never scream, you hardly speak but you play your records, don't you?

LV You're drunk you.

In the blackness, we hear the sound of **Mari** *smashing things around.*

Mari And you put out the damn stinking lights, don't you?

Suddenly lights come up and **LV** *is at the fusebox on a chair. Record player in her room suddenly whirrs back into life, Shirley Bassey record very loud.*

Mari (*almost falling over*) Shut that up! Stop it! Get it off! Get it!

LV *runs upstairs fast. She gets in her room, takes it off. Begins putting another one on.*

Mari Come down.

LV *doesn't answer.*

Mari Okay, stay up. Play your old records. Bore me. Make me want to be sick all over the house.

Pause.

Mari Hey, hey, this better not cock up the putting in of my new phone tomorrow. It won't, will it?

LV No.

Mari Goodoh for that.

Mari *stands in living room tottering. Suddenly, record from* **LV**'s *room really loud (Judy Garland, 'Come Rain or Come Shine'). She turns, feels sick, suddenly rushes to kitchen sink. Retching but nothing happening. She slides and knocks all the pans and plates off the side. Collapses on the kitchen floor.* **LV** *comes running downstairs. Music still playing loud. Helps* **Mari** *up. They stumble together.* **LV** *manages to get her back to the settee. They fall together on that.* **LV** *is trapped underneath her but manages to get out. She rolls her over on settee and tucks* **Mari**'s *coat around her, takes off* **Mari**'s *shoes, places them carefully. Covers* **Mari**'s *ears with pillows. Starts to go upstairs.* **Mari** *moans and mumbles.* **LV** *stops, turns back, then carries on up.* **LV** *goes in her room. Turns the record player up even louder. Listens awhile. Bam. Electricity blows again.*

LV Not again.

Blackout.

Lights up. Living room. Morning.

A **Man** *and a very tall younger man (*Billy*) from the phone company are fitting in a phone. They have baggy overalls on.* **Mari** *in dressing gown. Smoking. Watching them.*

Mari Is it nearly in now?

Phone Man Nearly in.

Mari I'll be in touch with the world soon. I can't believe it, I'll be wired up to all parts.

Phone Man You will, love.

Mari Goodly. I spend my life and my fortune in them slot boxes, really I do.

The **Phone Man** *stands up.*

Mari Oh, them uniforms are not very becoming. You look like you've been thrown in a tool bag.

Phone Man *laughs.*

Mari It's put me right off that. And I always liked a man in uniform too.

Phone Man I bet you did.

Mari Eh, watch it Sparks, Sparkeler. Eh, speaking of sparks, you don't know nothing about electrickery do you? The wires of me home is crackling up on me.

Phone Man No, I'm just a phone chap.

Mari And a good un I hope. How we doing?

Phone Man Almost there.

Mari He's quiet in' he? (*Indicating tall one.*)

Phone Man He is.

Mari Is there anybody there? (*Laughs.*) Has he been disconnected? My daughter's like that.

Phone Man Speak to her, Bill.

Billy Hi.

Mari Eh, you're not the famous phone bill, are you?

They laugh.

Mari I'm on form this morning, bloody Nora. I'm excited you see. Hey, don't think I'm tight or anything not offering tea, but you see how I want the job done as quick as possible don't you. I want voices. And also I'm expecting a call, if you know what I mean.

Phone Man *laughs.*

Mari You do, don't you? Look at you though in that bag. You ought to complain. I might phone and complain for you. Good looking on the top, then that. Clark Gable in a bag, or should I say Clark Cable.

She laughs, then suddenly sings, excited.

'Oh, give me a phone where the phoneolohs phone.' Hurry up lads.

Phone Man *hands* **Billy** *a hammer.* **Billy** *turns to put it in toolbag.*

LV *enters from stairs.* **Billy** *drops hammer.* **LV** *jumps.*

Billy (*shy*) Sorry.

They both bend to pick it up. She picks it up first, gives it to him, half smiles.

Mari Oh, look at them two looking now. Hey, he doesn't speak as well. You could go out together and have a silent night, holy night.

LV *goes back upstairs.*

Mari Eh, what did I say? What did I say? And look at the red of him now, looky. Oh dear.

Suddenly music comes on loud again from upstairs.

Hang on, that's all you get when she's upset, crappaty records, full blast.

She hits the ceiling with something.

Mari Cull it!

The music goes down.

Phone Man Right madam, it's done, I'll just ring through to test the line.

Mari Oh, let me. Let me, go on.

Phone Man Okay.

He passes phone to her.

Mari Oh, this virgin blower and coil, this spanking plastic, this phone of mine, Right, what's the number?

Phone Man 76543

Mari 7 . . . Oh, you press, I'll dialogue.

He does, she speaks.

Mari Hiyah love, we're on. Yes. Yes. PC Phone said I could ring you. Put me down on the chart. Bye.

She puts phone down. **Phone Man** *holds out a sheet and a pen.*

Phone Man Okay, could you sign this please. Er . . .?

She takes sheet.

Mari Mrs Hoff. Mari Hoff. (*As she takes pen.*) Crappaty name in' it? My late husband, Frank, left it me. (*As she signs.*) You can imagine my feelings on signing the marriage register, Mr and Mrs F Hoff.

Phone Man Aye. (*Laughs.*)

She picks up the phone again.

Mari See you now.

Phone Man See you.

Mari (*dialling*) Thank you Clark Cable, byeoh.

They are leaving.

Billy (*quiet*) See you.

She ignores him. He takes a last glance upstairs, leaves. **Mari**
through on phone.

Mari Hello. Auntie Slit, is that you? It's Mari. I knew
you'd be up. You're doing the dogs, aren't you? Yes,
I'm just phoning to say, I'm phoneable now. Yeah I
have the phone, the phone. The line through. Yes. No.
No. I'm not going in work today . . . Not really ill shall
we say. No. NOT ILL, NO. (*To herself.*) Bloody hell.
Alright, I'm ill.

LV *enters down the stairs. Picks up newspaper. Heads for
kitchen.*

Mari No, our LV's looking after me. (*To* **LV**.) Aren't
you, love? Yes. She's fine. (*To* **LV**.) Come and have a
word with Auntie Slit! She won't. Oh, is that them
barking. Right you go Auntie, you go out and cut the
meats. Yes, bye now. Woof woof.

Puts phone down.

Deaf old clit. (*To* **LV**.) Make us a cuppa, love. Look
after me. Give us that paper. (**LV** *does.*) Oh take it
back, I don't like the front. What a thing to wake up to,
dying, lying and destruction.

She picks up phone again.

LV I hope you've paid for that.

Mari Oh shut up, it's me new toy and in fact me
lifeline. Okay? Live while you can, that's my motto and
your lesson (*Through on the phone.*) Hello, hiyah. Did I
wake you? Ooh get out of it. I bet you never slept last
night. I bet you. I do. I bet you. Just dinging to say
I've got one in, a phone you sex fiend, 61815. Burn it
between your breasts. Anyway, I'm going now. Got to
keep the line free. You know how it is when you're
expecting the call . . . Yes, he brought me home, he

sure did, but that's all you're getting till later. Phone in
for the next thrilling instalment. Tell Mo and Licky but
no one else. Bye, Marmainia. See see see ya. Leg over
and out.

Puts phone down. **LV** *is sitting at kitchen table.*

Mari Shove us some food on something, LV. Go on,
slap some food about for me, love. Come on.

LV There is none.

Mari Please don't tell me that.

Mari *gets up, goes to kitchen looking for food. She bangs her
hand on kitchen table.*

Mari Oh, you're a misery you. Buck up will you.

LV *spills her drink.* **Mari** *returns to search.*

Mari What did you do last night?

LV *doesn't answer.*

Mari Play your records.
Play your records.
Bloody shit.

Mari *still searching for food.*

Mari You wanna live a bit.

LV Like you, you mean. The Merry Widow.

Mari Can't hear you. You'll have to speak up, Little
Voice. That's all we ever said when you was a kid. (*Still
looking for food.*) No bacon? I can't start the day without
some dribbling fat. Can you? What you eating, a brown
envelope?

LV A Ryvita.

Mari What, are you still a vegetarian?

LV *nods.*

Mari Oh yes. I forgot. (*Still looking for food.*) I'll tell you what, if there was a squealer in here, I'd chop it meself. Cut, cut.

She leaves kitchen, comes back into the living room.

Mari What's on the telly? (*Turns it on, turns it off before it even comes on.*) Oh sod that. Oh sod this, I'm going down the caf'. But first, ring, phone, ring. Give us paper while I'm waiting.

LV *passes it to her.*

Mari (*looks at her*) Why are you so miserable?

LV *ignores her.*

Mari Hey and listen you. I've been meaning to have a word with you for sometime about something. You never speak, right, you never leave the house. I want to know once and for all, are you agraphobical? Because if you are, you can get out.

LV I'm not.

Mari Right then. (*Reads on.*)

Mari *sits on sofa.*

Mari Come on cock, please brew.

LV *ignores her.*
Mari *throws newspaper up.*

Mari Bloody hell. Bloody hell, eh?

Knock at door.

Mari Come in, Sadie.

A great big fat woman comes in. The neighbour.

Mari Sit down. Crush a chair anywhere you like.

Sadie Okay.

Mari Do you want a cuppa or 'owt?

Sadie Okay.

Mari Make us one while you're at it.

Sadie Okay.

Mari Where am I this morning, the Okay Corral or what? Frig me. Don't put loads of bloody sugar in yours an all. You emptied half the bloody bag yesterday. (*Looks at the page of newspaper still left in her lap.*) Frig me up and down, look what's happened in the news.

Sadie What?

Mari She's named him and he didn't know.

She throws it away.

Do you like me phone?

Sadie (*looking*) Okay that.

Mari Okay! Wait 'til it starts trilling. In fact we shouldn't have long to wait as I'm expecting a call this morning.

Sadie (*excited*) A chap?

Mari On the nail, Sade.

LV *stands to leave.*

Mari Where you going?

LV *just makes her way upstairs.*

Mari Don't start that bloody music again. I've no head for that. (*To* **Sadie**.) Can you hear it next door?

Sadie At times, when I'm pegging out.

Mari (*to* **LV**) Did you hear that. (*To* **Sadie**.) Bloody crazed chil' she is. I'm sure it's that player what's sucking up all my 'tricity and causing sparks. Go on off upstairs like an ignorant. She bugs me at times. Though I'm all she's got and she's all I've got, besides me arse and tits. Where's that brew.

LV *puts a record on. It plays.* **Mari** *throws something at ceiling beneath* **LV**'s *room.*

Mari Cull it!

LV *turns it down. She gently puts her head on the player.*

Mari I don't know what to do with her. She's morbidity itself, just plays them damn records her Dad left her, over and a over. Just them, nothing else, on and on. That's not health is it, Sade? But what can I do? You can only do so much, can't you Sade?

Sadie *brings really steaming tea over.*

Sadie You can. You said chap?

Mari Oh yes . . . yes. (*Takes tea.*) Tar. Let me see yours. (**Sadie** *shows*.) I can see the sugar! Will you stop that.

Sadie Okay.

Mari Go on, drink it now.

They both sip.

Mari Well, Sadie, what a night! What-a-night! What a championship neet! In fact come here and belt me. Calm me down with a smack sandwich so I can tell the tale. Belt me.

Sadie *comes over and hits* **Mari**'s *two cheeks simultaneously.*

Mari Tar. Well, I copped off again with that Ray. I did it again. He had no choice. You couldn't have got a bar between us last night, I became his side. I was eye to eye with him all night. There was virtually only enough virtual room to move our drinks table to gob. The turn was a romantic singer, thank frig, and the music was in our heads, in our heads and in his wandering hands. Everyone's coming up to Ray allt' time, 'Howdo', 'Alright'. He knows so many people and I'm on his arm and his hands on my arse as he speaks to them. My arse. My golden old arse in Ray Say's hands. You can see how I am there. A queen. Queen for the night. He motored me home about a million miles an hour. I don't know what kinda car it is. One o'them big ones that bloody go, pistols in the back, all that, toaster in the dashboard, lights blinking on and off, put me up, put me down, put me up, put me down seats, thick as beds. Crack oh round the bloody roads we was. Heart in mouth, hand on leg, the lot. Then screeching to a halt outside, did you not hear us? You must be dead if you didn't. I saw every other curtain in the bitching road twitch. Then he comes at me with this pronto snog, lip-lapping like hell. That's men for you in it Sade, if you can remember. Lip-a-lapping, like old hell he was. But at least he's a lot better than most, at least he knows how to slide and dart and take a throat. At least there's always the thick wad of his wallet up against your tit for comfort.

Sadie Aye.

Mari *picks up a piece of newspaper.*

Mari Have you seen the headlines on the paper, look. Slavering, slavering. Men are always slavering. Only joking. You can't read, can you Sade?

Sadie I can get by, if the print's of a size.

Mari I know what you mean. You were a dab hand on the betting slips though, weren't you? When you had your trouble though, weren't you? In fact, he works on the tracks, Ray.

Sadie Is he a bookie?

Mari Sure. Besides having a finger in a load of other pies. Some too scorching bloody burning hot for his own good if you get my mean. In fact, he's moving into artist's management at the moment, you know. Yes. He's got Trigger Smit and Elaine, The Trumpet 4, Flaggy the Cot Poodle, and a couple of strippers at the moment. But he'll make it, he'll make it in anything, Ray Say. He's one o'them, give him an inch, he'll take the coal shed, how can I say, a lovable twat sort of type. (*Sips.*) See, partly partly, no, mainly mainly, that's why I got the (*Indicating phone.*) ragbone in. I've got to be on call. It's got to be smooth for him going out with me. I must win him. I've got to keep him. He's got a lot of young bitches into him a quart my age. I know they haven't got my wizzle and mince but I'm taking no chances Sade, how can I at my time of strife?

Music comes on loud again.

Mari Oh trash that calypso!

It goes down again.

Mari I've got to eat though or I won't be able to hold my own with him down the blower. Must be quick though, I'll phone and warn them. (*Rings cafe off a card she has, gets through.*) Caf-Caf, are you open? Right I'm coming down. In me slippers. I want Crackerbarrell on toast and a fuck hot tea. Tar. (*Puts phone down.*)

Sadie *gets up to leave.*

Mari While you're at the door get me me coat.

Sadie *does and holds it for her,* **Mari** *slips it on.* **Sadie** *goes out.* **Mari** *shouts upstairs.*

Mari I'm going down the caf'. If anyone phones before I return, this is more important than your life girl, tell them I'll be back in five minutes. Tell them that and that's all, alright? ALRIGHT? Are you receiving me?

LV (*from bedroom*) Yes.

Mari Toodle pip.

She leaves. The music is turned up full, ('I who have nothing', Shirley Bassey). **LV** *emerges from bedroom, comes downstairs. Music playing loud. She goes in kitchen. She opens fridge door, looks in.*

LV Oh God.

Closes it. Fills and plugs kettle in. Goes and picks pieces of newspaper up, tidies a little. Phone rings. She looks at it, scared. Looks at it. Lowers her hand over it. Retreats. Runs upstairs, turns off record player. Peeps down, it's still ringing. Comes down, frightened. Suddenly, a knock at the door. She looks at door. Knock again. She opens it. It is the shy phone boy, **Billy**.

Billy (*shy*) Hello, I put your phone in.

She nods.

Billy I think we left our hammer.

She looks, sees it, nods. Steps back to let him in.

Billy Oh.

He goes to get it. It's by the phone. He gets it.

Billy Your phone's ringing.

She nods. Looks at it. He can see she's uncomfortable.

Billy Do you want me to get it for you?

She nods. He picks it up.

Billy Er . . . Mari . . . Er . . .

LV She's gone Caf-Caf.

Billy What?

LV Back soon.

Billy She will be back soon. Right. Right.

Puts phone down.

Ray, he'll ring back.

LV Thanks.

Billy (*clutching hammer*) Yes. (*Not knowing what to say.*) I don't like talking on phones an' all. An' I work with 'em.

She nods. They look at each other. He wants to say more, but can't.

Billy See you then.

He goes to leave. Stops.

Billy See you.

LV *nods. He leaves. She closes door. Kettle explodes.*

Blackout.

Lights up.

Living room, night. **LV** *is sitting in dark. TV on, light flickering up her face, an old Judy Garland film.*

Door suddenly bursts open.

Mari *there. Switches light on.*

Mari Right you. You've got a fucking second to get in shape.

Runs from back, leaps over the settee. Turns TV off. Goes back round towards door.

Mari Perk girl perk. (*At door.*) Aye come in Ray. Come in. Here he is (*She holds her hand towards door.*) Mr Ray Say.

Man comes in, forties, in a suit, hair quiffed slightly.

Mari Here it is, my home. My phone. My kitchen. My wall. My telly. My daughter.

Ray How do.

Mari Ray. Sun Ray. Sting Ray. Ray Gun. My Ray of hope. I'm a frigging just inta him so. (*She kisses him. To* **LV**.) Well, say hello at least. You miserable spot. I've warned you.

LV (*awkward, almost inaudible*) Hello.

Mari Oh, she's a miserable misery. What you having Raymondo and don't say nowt rude, ha!

Ray What's in?

Mari Everything your throat could desire.

She suddenly speeds round house collecting half empty bottles and standing them in the middle of the room. One from under a table. One from behind a cushion. One from the washing machine. One from under the telly. At one point she makes **LV** *stand up while she looks under the settee for a bottle, it rolls out. She assembles them all in the middle of the floor.*

Mari There.

Ray I'll have a cup of tea, tar.

Mari You'll what? (*Laughing.*) He'll have a cup o'tea. Har. Ha ha he. (*Looks at LV.*) Look, look, she nearly laughed then, din't you eh? Nearly.

LV *stands up and heads for her bedroom.*

Mari Hey, don't just go like that, you rude slit. Hey!

Ray Leave her, she's alright.

Mari No. It's not right, she spoils everything, her. I'm trying to make an impression and she can't even be swivel to a friend. The little tiny slit!

She kicks a chair over, boots the bottles.

Mari Oh what am I doing and in front of you! Oh well, that's it, I give up. This is my crappaty home, and this is how I am Ray, no gracey airs, and if you don't like it piss off out of it.

Ray Hey, hey, calm down. Don't get mad at me. I didn't say anything about anything.

Mari Oh okay, come on, let's roll about.

She pulls him on settee. His drink goes flying. They snog and roll about.

Suddenly, from above, the sound of Judy Garland loud, 'The man that got away.

Ray What's that?

Mari I'll shut her up.

Ray Leave it.

Mari *hits ceiling again.*

Mari Cull it!

The music doesn't go down. Angry. She starts to go upstairs.

Mari Right!

Ray Hey, hey, never mind. Come on. Come here.

Mari (*stops*) Ha. You're right. Sod the bitch. We'll have our own on.

She goes to radiogram, puts her own record on. Turns it up. Both are going now. She goes back to **Ray***. They roll about snogging. Suddenly the lights go. The electrics have gone again.* **Ray** *stops. The two record players grind to a halt.*

Mari You've blown me fuse.

They laugh and carry on. **LV** *begins singing 'The man that got away' from where the record left off. It sounds just like the record. The song continues for some time.* **Ray** *and* **Mari** *snogging. Then suddenly* **Ray** *stops.*

Ray How can that be, has she a radio?

Mari That's not 'her', that's her.

Ray What?

Mari I mean, that's not the record, that's LV.

Ray No.

Mari Yeah.

Ray No.

Mari Yeah.

Ray No.

Mari Fucking hell.

Ray That's her singing, but that's amazing.

Mari Amazin' Ray sin. Come on, let's roll about.

Ray Hold on. How can she do that?

Mari I don't know, throat twisting, I presume. Roll.

Ray I still don't believe it.

Mari Look, Ray, she plays 'em all the time, every God sented sec'. They're stuck in her head. She can sing them. It gets on my wick. End of story. Come on. I'm ready.

Ray Where did she get them?

Mari When he died, he left them her.

Ray Your husband?

Mari Yeah, Frank.

Ray What was he like then?

Mari Put it this way, he listened to women's records.

Ray So.

Mari Put it this way. He was thin and tall and hardly spoke. When I was a teenager, I thought I'd found Gary Cooper but ended up I'd found Olive Oil. He was a length of dry stick that bored me bra-less. He sat folded up in that chair there resembling misery in its many fucking forms and he tried to make me the same. He could not succeed. Come on lover boy.

Ray (*still towards the singing*) Hang on, I'm listening.

Mari Come on, lover boy, I'm contorted here.

Ray Ssssh. Hold on.

Mari Oh, I'm off then.

She closes her eyes and immediately falls asleep. **Ray** *listens intently till the song ends. Then he starts clapping.*

LV, *upstairs, afraid.*

Blackout.

Living room/kitchen. Morning

LV *comes downstairs, goes in kitchen. Opens bread bin. Takes out a curled crust of white bread from the bottom of it. She is heading for toaster with it.* **Ray** *appears from stairs, pulling on* **Mari***'s dressing gown over bare chest and trousers.*

Ray Hi.

She drops the precious piece of bread.

Ray Don't get a shock, it's only me, Ray Say, remember.

She doesn't speak, goes to plug in kettle. It flashes. She jumps again.

Ray You wanna watch that. Could fetch the house down. And so could you with what you did last night.

LV *retreats further into kitchen, bit afraid. Gets a glass of water.*

Ray Bloody marvellous that. Who else do you do, eh?

She starts to go.

Ray Don't go. I'm interested cause I'm showbusiness meself you see. R Say very personal management. Your mam must have told you. No? Well never mind. (*Indicating bread.*) Shame about the crust cock, here let me rustle you up one of Ray Say's famous breakfassays. I do 'em all the time for my artistes, when we's on a foreign engagement. Not all glamour our game you know.

He opens fridge.

Oh God.

Closes it quick.

Ray You ever bin to Spain?

LV No.

Ray Last weekend I flew a couple of the girls and myself out to do a show. I know an old jockey runs a bartello there, 'The Princess Di', good gig, good gig. Bloody mad out there though. Raging, love, wild. Not like the postcards. I've got two scars somewhere I brought back for souvenirs. One on me chest, see. And one on me lip, look. (*He gets close, she looks.*) Can I just say again while you're this close. Bloody marvellous what you did last night. Marvellous in the dark there, something I'll never forget. Do you mind if I ask you something love?

LV *shakes her head.*

Ray How the hell on earth do you do it?

LV Uh, I . . .

Ray No, no, don't try. Don't. You wouldn't know. The true performer never does, take it from me. I understand the artiste, you see. Do you know Wild Trigger Smit and his good lady Elaine. I'm the only one in showbiz who can handle him. She thinks the sun shines out of me, Elaine, especially now I've got him off the knives and back on vocals. He were on 'Opportunity Knocks' in '69, you know. They say he would a won but he butted the make-up man or summat. He's not like that now though old Trig'. (*As he turns to shelves.*) Thank frig.

He casually pulls a packet of cornflakes down, looks in.

Ray What's this, a box of privet leaves, urgh they's all green.

He puts them back.

Ray I'll tell you what, what say you and me continue our conversation down the Caf-Caf.

LV No thanks.

Ray (*surprised*) No . . . I'll pay and everything.

Gets his fat wallet out.

LV No.

Ray Okay, suit yourself.

LV But.

Ray Yeah.

LV Er . . .?

Ray Hey fire away love.

LV In showbusiness, did you ever meet Shirley Bassey?

Ray Now then . . . Shirley, to be honest no love, our paths have never crossed. I've met Monkhouse though. (*Sees she's not impressed.*) And of course Cilla.

LV Cilla?

Ray Yeah.

LV No.

Ray Sure.

LV (*eager*) What's she like?

Ray Alreet.

LV I've got one of hers upstairs.

Ray You can't do her an' all can you?

He starts putting his wallet away. While he's distracted and not looking, she speaks in a Cilla-type voice.

LV Hello, do you know who this is Ray?

Ray *turns white.*

Ray (*seriously shocked*) Christ, I can't believe that. Take it from me. Hey . . . Hey. Honest love. Take it from me . . . Does no one know about this?

LV No. (*Shakes her head.*)

Ray I can't believe it. What does your Mam say?

LV Nowt.

Ray Nowt?

LV No.

Ray Listen seriously LV. Listen, you are my discovery. I've found you right, me, always remember that. In fact here, have one o'me new cards. (*He gets one out.*) Gold, look.

She is fascinated by the glint of it, but won't take it.

Ray No, here you are, you're the first to have one a these.

She almost takes it, but doesn't.

Ray No, there love. I wouldn't give one a these to everyone.

She takes it.

Ray Now listen LV. I know you're quiet, your Mam's told me that, but together you and me we could set the place on fire.

LV You're a nutter you.

She goes.

Ray And you're a star.

She goes upstairs.

Ray, *excited, runs to phone. Dials.*

Ray Hello! Hello, is Mr Boo in, I need to speak to him now . . . It's Ray Say, Say, Say, yeah. No, it can't wait, no. Hold him there. I'm coming down now!

He puts phone down, starts off upstairs to finish dressing. Half way up he meets **Mari** *coming down, looking crap.*

Ray Marrii!

Mari Don't speak to me. Don't speak for a minute.

Ray *laughs and continues upstairs.*

Mari *comes down. She goes in kitchen area hunting for an aspirin. She finds one. Then can't find a cup in all the mess on the draining board.*

Mari Cup cup.

Knocks something off draining board.

Mari Aarrrgh!

Drops aspirin into an empty milk bottle. Puts water in. While it's dissolving, she holds her head at the sound it's making. Drinks it.

Ray *reappears, bounding downstairs, putting on tie. Jacket over arm.*

Mari Darling, how are you?

Goes to embrace him. **Ray** *is dressing as he speaks.*

Ray I've got to dash Mari. But what can I say? It's happened at last, eh! I'm so excited, it's like at the races when you've found yourself a little nag no one's noticed but you know you're onto a certainty and you're feeling, this is it! She is the one. Do you know what I mean?

A knock on the door.

Mari Go on, yes! Yes! I'm with you lad. Yes . . .

Ray It's like . . .

Mari Yeah. Yeah. (*Desperate.*) Ignore that.

It's too late, **Ray** *is opening it. It's* **Billy**.

Billy It's, er, me again. Er, just come to see if your phone's still alright.

Mari *snatches handset up. Holds it out to him.*

Mari Is that its sound?

Billy Yes.

Mari It's reet!

Slams door.

Mari On Ray, on.

Ray (*forgetting where he was*) Er . . .

Mari You were under starters orders and you were off!

Ray Yeah. It's not just my future, it's yours.

Mari Oh my God.

Ray I still can't believe it. It's what I've been looking for for ages. And here it is under this roof, under me very nose. All I can say is . . .

Knock on door. **Rays** *opens it.*

Mari No, leave it! For Godsake leave it!

Sadie *is standing there.*

Ray (*as he leaves*) I'll be back soon. I can't leave it. Not this. Best to act fast when you're this sure eh?

Mari *nods frantically.*

Ray It's just one o'them once in a lifetime things.

He passes **Sadie** *and leaves.* **Mari** *takes her by the sleeve and silently draws her in the house.*

Mari Sadie, did you hear that utterance? Did you? Did you hear what Say sayeth. It were almost on the tip there of his raspberry tongue, he wants me. I can't believe it Sade. The bastard wants me. Get Jackson 5 on, Sadie. We always play it when we've something to celebrate, don't we?

Sadie, *happy, runs to radiogram and gets it on.*

Mari At last. At last. Saved, secured. I shall go to the ball. Oh darlings from the sky.

The music comes on: 'I want you back' Jackson 5. They dance all around the room. Music blaring. They dance till they have to stop.

Mari Oh, oh stop. I can't breathe.

Sadie *turns it off. They collapse on settee and chairs.*

Mari Din't I say to you though Sadie, when I first spied him, I knew there was summat down for us. I just had that twat-bone feeling, and you know me, I can predict rain with that.

She suddenly gets up.

Hey, I'd better get dressed up, who knows when he will return. Where's me knickers and bra?

Pulls some out the washing basket, they are all tangled up with a line of other bras and knickers and suspender belts and tea towels etc. She can't separate them.

(*Speaking as she tries.*) I'm one high razzamatazza in here today. (*Hitting her chest.*) It's like there's a circus parade passing over my paps. What a life, life can be.

In the end she just takes them all up in a long trail. She heads for the stairs trailing them all behind her.

(*As she ascends.*) Sadie, make yourself a cup of sugar with some tea in it. I shall be down shortly.

She goes upstairs and into her room, slams door. **Sadie***, still panting, goes into kitchen to make tea.*

LV *alone in her room. Suddenly, we see a yellow 'Cherry Picker' (platform on a winch, used by telephone engineers and for lighting maintenance on lamp-posts etc.) coming high round the side of house.* **Billy** *is in it, holding a hammer.*

It comes along alley and up level with her window. **LV** *screams.* **Billy** *speaks.*

Billy Just seeing if wires are alright.

She looks at him amazed. Can't hear him through the window.

Billy (*louder*) Just seeing if wires are alright!

She opens window.

Billy Just seeing! . . .

Nearly knocks her over with shout, quickly quietens.

Billy . . . if wires are alright.

Starts whistling. Whistling as he looks at wall, up and down.

Billy Do you go out much?

LV No.

Billy *whistling.*

Billy Are you a telly fan?

LV No.

Billy *whistling. Presses button, goes out to side a bit, away from her view.*

Billy Are you going anywhere for your holidays?

LV No.

Whistling trails off.

Billy There are no wires.

LV Eh?

Billy I should be up a telegraph pole three streets away, but I come here.

Presses button, returns to window.
They look at each other.

Billy I don't know what to say now.

Pause. They look at each other.

Billy I'm like this at work. Then when I do speak they all jump like I've dropped a brick in a bucket.

He smiles nervously. She does a bit.

Billy I'm Billy. Can I ask you your name.

LV LV.

Billy Oh, does that stand for something?

LV Little Voice.

Billy Oh, cause of your soft voice.

LV I think it's more cause no one could never hear me.

Billy I can.

Pause.

Billy Your Mam's a live wire in't she. Bloody hell.

LV Aye.

Billy I live with me Grandad. It's quiet in our house, the clock an all that.

LV Ours is a mad house.

Billy Aye. (*Pause.*) Hope you don't mind having a chat this high up.

LV No, do you?

Billy No. No. Safe as houses these. It goes higher than this, this. See.

He presses a button. Machine rises to above the roof height.

Billy I like going up. Better view.

LV What view?

Billy (*looking*) Backs. Backs. Works. Works. Backs. Works. Backs. And the last chimney.

LV I can't even see that.

Billy No, your view's blocked by Vantona.

LV Me Mam works there.

Billy Oh aye. Maybe I can see her through one of the little windows.

LV You won't. She hardly ever goes in.

Billy Oh.

He presses button, comes down. **LV** *stands up. They face each other.*

Billy Little Voice, I don't know what's come over me. I've not been able to rest till I could come here again.

I've only been like this once before. That's when I first
saw Blackpool illuminations.

Pause.

Billy Do *you* by any chance, like, by any chance, light
displays at all, LV? I only ask 'cause it's the one thing I
can really talk about and I don't want to dry up on
you, not now.

She smiles, confused. He takes this as permission to continue.

I've got me Grandad's shed on the allotment and I've
blacked out the windows. I . . . No, I'll say no more, it
can be boring to the non-enthusiast.

LV No, you're alright.

Billy You sure.

LV *nods.*

Inside that shed. Inside that shed. When I throw the
switch, Little Voice, you wun't believe it. Light. Up the
walls. Off the ceiling, caught light, bent light, beams
under beams of it, colours, colours coming up through
colours you've never seen. Shades to make you happy,
shades to make you sad, shades to make you Voom!

The last word he sent out so powerfully in his exitement **LV**
falls back in surprise.

Sorry!

LV No.

Billy So sorry.

LV It's alright.

Billy I don't know what it is, after the illuminations,
that was it. I'd only play with torches and Christmas

tree lights, I spent all me youth with the curtains closed, fascinated, helpless as a moth.

Pause.

Only thing is I'll never show. Me Grandad says I'm like an artist painting masterpieces and keeping them under the stairs, he keeps mythering me to do the lights for his pensioners' 'do' down the working man's club. I always say no. Somehow though, I don't know. After talking to you, telling you. Maybe I shall do it. I don't know. If I did would you come down?

LV I don't know. I don't go out.

Billy Would you think about it. I could go and find out all the details. I really would be honoured. I really would be so . . . If you could just see them, LV. (*Almost to himself.*) I'd take from above, I'd bring down some heaven. Poor old sods they'd think they were getting a mirror ball and a couple of spotlights and they'd be flying when I'd done.

Mari *comes out of her bedroom, stops on landing.*

Mari What's going on. You talking to yourself now gal!

LV (*to* **Billy**) Sorry. I got go.

She hurriedly closes window.

Mari Is that you and your voices.

Billy LV, the lights.

LV *is gone inside. He presses button, begins to disappear back round corner.*

Mari (*to herself*) Crazed.

Mari *comes grandly downstairs, tarted up.* **Sadie** *is in living room.*

Well, Sadie, how do I look? And don't say okay or I'll poke your Pilsbury dough.

Sadie *has a mouthful of something, so just nods approvingly.*

What you eating? I thought there was nothing in.

Sadie Cornflakes.

Mari Oh.

Suddenly, the sound of a car outside screeching up. **Mari** *looks out of window.*

Mari It's Ray Say. I didn't expect him so soon.

She rushes to mirror; lacquer can and sherry bottle at side. Starts lacquering and quick drinking in turn.

Mari Lacquer! Liquor! Lacquer! Liquor!

She lacquers all over her hair and everywhere fast.

Mari Oh I've had the colour shocked out of me.

Slaps both her cheeks hard.

Mari Come on up you young apples. You cheeky cheeks.

She looks out again.

Mari He's got someone wi' him. Maybe it's the vicar.

Sadie *stands up.*

Mari Don't take me serious, Sade. (*To herself.*) Fat sucker.

Sadie *sits again.*

Mari No, no, it's that bloke from the club, what the hell's he doing with him? Come on, Sadie, sod off. I need some seats free. (*Changing her mind.*) No, no stay and get drinks.

Knock at door. **Mari** *opens it.* **Ray** *and* **Mr Boo** *step in.*

Mari Darling, din' expect you back so swoon.

Ray Mari, you know Mr Boo from down the club.

Mr Boo Call me Lou.

Billy (*almost curtsying*) Pleasured I'm sure, Mr Lou.

Ray No, Lou's his first name.

Mari (*almost curtsying again*) Sorry. Sit down.

Ray This is Little Voice's mother.

Mari (*to* **Ray**) Hang on. Little Voice? What's going on?

Ray Like I said Mari, LV's a real discovery, a once in a lifetime thing. That's why I've dragged Mr Boo straight down here to hear her.

Mr Boo *nods.*

Mari LV?

Ray Yeah.

She goes away to her liquor bottle by mirror.

Ray Will you just get her down for us, cock, Mr Boo's not got long you see, have you?

Mr Boo (*looking at watch*) Nope.

Mari (*drinking*) You know where she rots. Fetch her yourself.

Ray (*goes upstairs a little. Softly*) LV! LV! It's Ray Say, remember? Can you come down love. I've brought someone to hear you do your stuff love?

Mr Boo *coughs.*

Ray Someone important LV love!

No response. He goes right up to **Mari.**

Ray Mari, will you go and get her?

Mari (*snaps at Ray*) You're tapped, you. She'll not sing in public, LV.

Ray Hey, I want Boo to hear her sing, alright?

Mari She'll not throat on cue, LV.

Mr Boo Everything alright, Say?

Ray Oh aye.

Mr Boo Just reminding you lad, I've not all day.

Ray Aye. (*To* **Mari.**) Listen, my reputation's at stake here, get up them dancers and get her down.

Mari Easier said than done.

Ray Listen Mari, I want her down. What's up with you?

Mari You.

Ray Eh?

Mari You with your 'special' and all that, the 'one and only' and all that. I thought you meant me din't I?

Ray (*struggling now*) Hey. I do. Bloody hell, Mari, I did. I do. Yes. You are special, bloody hell, you know that. I meant I found you both at the same time. That's what I meant. Eh? Course I did.

Puts his arm around her.

Ray Eh?

Mari Oooh you.

Mari *goes up close to* **Ray**, *almost kissing.*

Mari Elvis breath.

Ray Go on, get her down love.

Mari Well, anything for you love, but I think you've backed your first loser there Ray, sorry to say.

She goes to stairs. Stops on first step, looks over to **Sadie** *and* **Mr Boo**. **Mr Boo** *reading newspaper.* **Sadie** *staring out.*

Mari Sadie talk to Lou Boo.

Carries on upstairs to **LV**'s *room.*

Sadie Okay. (*To* **Mr Boo**.) Hello.

Mr Boo Hi.

Sadie *just turns back to looking out.* **Mr Boo** *glares over at* **Ray**.

Ray (*to* **Mr Boo**) Won't be a minute now Mr Boo.

Mr Boo *cracks out the paper and reads again.*

Mari LV. LV.

LV *is inside, album covers all around her and up in front of her face as she reads the back of one.* **Mari** *goes in.*

Mari Come down, Ray wants you a minute.

She doesn't reply.

Mari Ray wants you for a minesota, will you get
down?

LV What for?

Mari You know what for, you've got him thinking you
can do summat or summat. He wants you down
anyway, show some showman or summat.

LV It's private.

Mari Private, my privates. You're just damn selfish
and useless and can do nowt but whisper and whine
like your Father before you, a couple of nowts.

LV *turns away, behind record sleeve.*

A load of dirty auld discs and a clapped out player.
The sum of your Father's life. Just a load of old rubbish
nobody wants.

LV *covers her ears.* **Mari** *snatches LP cover from her.* **LV** *gets
it back.*

LV Don't dare ever touch these.

Mari Up yours, stick leg.

She goes out and downstairs to **Ray**.

Mari (*on her way down*) She won't come down.

Ray What?

Mari Just as I told you, she won't sing, told you.

Mr Boo What's happening, Say?

Ray She's not quite prepared yet, Mr Boo, late sleeper
and all that, see.

Mr Boo Well I've gotta be off. Sorry and all that, Say. Maybe some other time, eh.

Ray Hold on.

Mr Boo (*to* **Sadie**) Goodbye er . . .

Sadie Sadie May.

Mr Boo Sadie May, nice to make your acquaintance. Bye all.

Starts to leave. **Ray** *goes after him.*

Ray Mr Boo wait. I'm sure we can persuade her. Hold on, give me a minute. I'll get her down. Believe me Boo! It's like I said.

Mr Boo's *out.* **Ray**'s *out after him.* **Mari** *follows on.* **Sadie** *after. Door slams.*

Mr Boo Hard to tell when I've heard nowt.

Mari Leave it Ray.

Ray (*to* **Mr Boo**) Come back inside.

Mr Boo Enough's enough. I've got to get back down the club.

Ray Look, you know me. I wouldn't fetch you down here for nowt. You've got to hear her. I can sort it, you know me.

LV *upstairs has heard the door slam. She sits on her bed, sings to herself. 'Never Never' (Shirley Bassey). Suddenly voices outside subside to silence.*

Ray *appears from corner of building listening and stands under lamp-post.*

Mr Boo *comes next and joins him. Then* **Mari** *and last*
Sadie. *They cluster under the lamp, almost like carol singers,*
listening. She sings a couple of verses. Stops.

Ray That was her.

Mr Boo Wasn't.

Ray Was.

Mr Boo Wasn't.

Ray Was.

Mr Boo No.

Ray Yes.

Mari (*to herself*) Here we fucking go again.

LV *starts to sing again. Changes song to 'Somewhere over the*
Rainbow' (Judy Garland) sings some, then hums softly.

Ray That was her an all.

Mr Boo Well, it's remarkable that. You have a
remarkable daughter there, Mrs Hoff.

Mari Thank you, I'm sure.

Mr Boo Well, Ray, we must have her if you can
arrange it. There's the makings of a class act there,
class. We could do a lot with that.

Ray It'll cost you.

Mr Boo I expected it to.

Ray Come on, Mr Boo.

They start to leave.

Ray (*to* **Mari**) We're off to talk fine details and
finances.

Mari (*following*) I'm with you. Don't forget me. The flesh and blood management.

LV *picks up song again.* **Sadie** *left standing alone below lamp, cheek on hands, rapt.* **LV** *finishes song, totally unaware of what's taking place.*

Blackout.

Night. Living room.

Mari *and* **Ray** *come in, drunk.* **Ray**'s *tie down. They sit on settee.*

Mari Roll about. Roll about.

They do. She flings her arms about.

Mari Roll about me.

They continue.

Mari Eh, eh. I'm going to get the little star up and tell her the news. Where am I?

She stands.

Mari Shove me in the right direction.

Ray Arrgh, leave it to the morning.

Mari No no. It might change her little life, this. Might bloody change mine for once. I never thought anyone would want to see her. Never in a million.

Ray Sometimes what's under your nose, you don't smell. It's the way of it.

Mari I know, I know. You have a wisdom, Ray. Also, you know what to say in many situations, also you know how to have a laugh, dress and drive. Also you have a fair sized dong. I'm glad I made your acquaintance.

Ray I'm going for a slash.

Tottering to stairs, she goes up. **Ray** *follows her and goes in toilet. She taps on* **LV***'s door, goes in.* **LV** *is asleep.* **Mari** *looks at her, stumbles, reaches to wake her, then stops. Stumbles, sits on bedside. Reaching out again but gently strokes her hair. Tucks her in. Suddenly* **Ray** *bursts in through door.*

Ray Alright! Well then! What does she think eh?

Mari *stumbles, falls off bed.* **LV** *wakes.*

LV Arrgh, what's . . . Aarrgh.

Mari Love, lovey, don't worry. It's me, me and Ray.

Ray Hiyah.

LV What do you want? What you doing?

Mari We've got some good news for you.

Ray Stupendous news actually like.

Mari Mr Boo, he's a man would like you to sing at the club, yes, on the stage.

Ray Sing what you like.

LV (*dumbstruck*) No, no.

Mari No, listen love. He'll pay. Yes, he will pay. Good money an all. Could be up to £50. Right Ray?

Ray Right and that's only the start of it.

LV No.

Mari Ray'll look after you, he knows all about it. And all you'll have to do is sing. Sing, what you like best doing anyways. Sing.

LV No, please.

Mari You might feel shy. I know what you're thinking.

Ray You might be shy at first.

Mari Natural that.

Ray I had a girl recently wouldn't say boo to a goose, now she's topping the bill at the Reform Club.

Mari Is that the stripper?

Ray Well, yes, but it's similar, int'it. Similar case, Tina.

LV Please go. Please. Please.

She pulls covers up around her, backs into corner like she's being hunted.

LV Please go. Please.

They go. Close door behind them and head downstairs.

Ray Bloody hell, I din' think she'd take it quite like that.

Mari Aye. Give her a while to let it sink in. Actually I'll go up, go up and have another word with her.

Ray (*takes hold of her*) No, no, you were right, leave it.

Mari What a hold you have on you, Ray, firm but fancy. Let's roll about once again.

They do. **LV** *above, still in corner with blankets grabbed to her.*

LV (*in a whisper*) Dad, Dad, Dad, Dad, Dad, Dad, Dad.

Below **Ray** *and* **Mari** *fall off settee.*

Mari I'm going go up and have a word with her. I feel
tight.

She stands up with difficulty and heads for stairs.

Ray Aye and I'm off an' all to rustle up some
champagne.

Mari At this time?

Ray Sure.

Mari Nowt's beyond you Ray is it? You're a bloody
genius in your own right.

Ray Hey, how about some takeaway an all.

Mari Ooh yeah. I'll have a Kwai Chang Caine with
curry, rice and chips.

Ray Okay. Hey, I wanna just be sure of one thing.
She'll be there, won't she Mari?

Mari Leave it wi' me Ray. I know her. I am her
mother after all.

Ray Soy sauce?

Mari *puts up the 'OK' sign.*

Ray *blows her a drunken kiss.* **Mari** *catches it and spreads it
all over her face and neck.*

He leaves. She goes upstairs.

LV *hears someone on the stairs. Quickly she throws pillow
under sheet like she's there, then runs out room and into
bathroom.* **Mari** *comes quietly into room, in dark, just
moonlight through window. She sits on end of bed.*

Mari I know you can't be asleep yet our LV, but I
won't make you sit up. I don't like forcing you into
something like this, I know it's against your nature,

but your Mam's sick of struggling, love. Sick to the bones with working and still having nowt. I'm thinking of you as well, you can't go on like this forever, stuck in your room, you're young. You have to do something with your life. This might bring you out, eh? Eh? You don't know what it could lead to, eh? You've always been a little voice and you've never liked much, to speak and such, but this thing you've developed could make us Ray reckons. Don't know where the hell it's come from, such a small quiet lonely thing you've always been. I could almost fit you in my two hands as a babe. (*Cups her two hands.*) I don't know if it's the drink but I keep seeing you tonight as our little LV there, little pale chil' in me arms, or in the old pram there, that lemon coloured crocheted blanket around you, tiny good-as-gold face in the wool. I'm sorry for the way I am love at times with you, it seems to be the way I am. It seems to be something . . . Anyway think on it, our LV. You will won't you, eh? Eh?

She reaches over and gently touches lump. Touches it again. Jumps up, pulls cover back. Grabs up cushion.

Mari　The little piss. I'll have her.

She head butts the cushion splitting it and sending feathers everywhere. **Ray** *enters below, bottle in one hand, takeaway in the other, slamming door.* **LV** *comes out from bathroom, then looks towards her room in fright.* **Mari** *spins round to see her, shouting through the feather fall.*

Mari　YOU ARE BLOODY DOING IT!

Blackout.

Interval.

Act Two

The club.

The organ and drums duo are playing frantically away at full blast.

Mr Boo *comes on, the music stops with a cymbals clash.*

Mr Boo Tar. Thank you. Tar. (*Indicates organist.*) Jean on her organ, ladies and gentlemen, Jean.

Mr Boo *applauds.* **Jean** *plays a riff.*

Mr Boo Jean, lovely. And Manolito, ladies and gentlemen, Manolito.

He plays a bit of drums. **Mr Boo** *applauds, riff continues as he speaks.*

Mr Boo Yes. Yes. Beat that meat, Manolito. Yes sir. Bad man, bad.

He does a little Michael Jackson dance. Manolito ends riff. **Mr Boo** *steps forward to audience.*

Mr Boo Yes. Here we are. Here we are then.

Mr Boo *at mike.*

Mr Boo Boo here. Don't shout my name too loud or I'll think you don't like me. How you all doing, alreet?! (*Waits for audience response.*) Come on you can do better than that. How you all doing?! Alreet. Great. Now then, now then, as you know, Boo braves anything, goes anywhere in his perpetual quest to hunt down fresh talent and lay it at your mercy. And you know how I've sweated, and you know how I've toiled, and you know how I've bent over backwards. (*To someone in* *audience*.) Watch it! And you know I've left no tonsil unturned in my unceasing search for something new on the vocal front. But for all that, I've found her round the corner, on the doorstep, at the kitchen table, she's so local I could spit and hit her. A talent, an undiscovered treasure. An act of wonder, ladies and gentlemen, something to thrill to, to spill beer or tears to, a little girl that's big, a northern light, a rising star, order and hush, hush and order, for the turn of turns. The one, the only, LITTLE VOICE! LITTLE VOICE!

Spotlight burning the stage. Microphone on stand. **Ray** *brings* **LV** *halfway on, directs her towards microphone, leaves. She comes into spot. She stands there. Quiet. Stands there. Quiet, trembling. Opens her mouth. Nothing. Upset.*

Ray's voice Lights, turn the lights out!

All the lights go out. She sings: Billy Holiday 'Lover Man'. Perfect impersonation. After a few lines, suddenly stops abruptly.

Ray's voice Do another, do another, more.

She does 'Chicago' Judy Garland. After a verse or so, again cuts off.

Ray's voice What you stopped for? Don't stop now. Do anything, anything.

She sings 'Happy Birthday' Marilyn Monroe. Finishes.

Ray's voice Get 'em back up! Back up!

Lights up. She is caught 'feeling it' then stunned like a frightened animal caught in headlights.

Blackout.

Lights up. Bam.

Back at house. **LV** *in her room.* **Mari** *downstairs, going frantically about the place throwing things over her shoulder, looking for something.*

Ray *at table, paper and pen out, working excitedly.*

Mari Embarrassing!

Throws something without looking. It just misses **Ray**, *who doesn't even respond, just ducks and carries on working.*

Mari Bloody one hundred chunk embarrassing that. I'm shown up. I'll never place my face in there again. Never, never. (*To* **Ray**.) Will you stop that scritching. I've just been involved with the worst spectacle and frig-up in Mari's history and you're crouched there scritching like a rat.

Ray I'm working on the act.

Mari Working on the act. Working on the act. Are you mental altogether? What act! There was only one sucker on show there tonight, me! Embarrassing. See her quavering in the dark there like a demic! See her! And what was she singing? What the hell was that? She could a made an effort and done Kylie for Christsake.

Ray Calm down.

Mari Calm down! You must be jesting. I'm up to me neck in shame.

Ray We had to find her limits. See what she could do.

Mari Nowt.

Ray No. The gold's there alright. I've just got to find me a way of fetching it out.

Mari Frig that. (*Returns to searching.*) Is there not a bottle nowhere?

Ray If the artiste won't go to the act, the act will have to go to the artiste. All's I have to do is think. Get my mind out, think.

Mari You should a thunk before. You wouldn't listen, would you? I told you and bloody Boo Lou, both, you were wasting your time on the slit. She did the whole thing on purpose to spite mother. I know her Ray. Oh my God, when she come on like that though. Oh my God. I din't know where to put meself. I still don't. Shame ran right up me leg.

Suddenly there's a sound like stones hitting a window. We see **Billy** *in the alley under the lamp, tossing little stones up to* **LV***'s window.*

Mari What's that? Is that in my head or on the outside?

Ray Eh? What? (*He listens.*) Outside.

Mari Bam me, funny business!

She bursts out of the house and sees **Billy***.*

Mari Clear off. Go on. Heated up pole. Piss it. Go.

He's gone. She throws stones after him. **Mari** *goes back in.*

Mari I'm too mad to live tonight.

She looks this way and that for something to grab. She turns on **Ray** *who's still working.*

Mari Anyway, stop that off! Cause she's not doing another. No way. Don't forget that's my diddy and delicate daughter you're twiddling wi'. And besides that there's my personal mother's nerves to consider!

He grabs her quickly by the wrist and pulls her onto his knee.

Ray (*quickly*) Come here. Calm down!

He starts tickling her up and down.

Ray Calm down. Calm down.

She starts hooting and laughing.

Mari Stop it. Oooooo. Stop it.

Ray (*tickling on*) You're calming down now, eh? Calming down now, eh?

He stops. She remains on his lap.

Ray You calmed down now, eh? Eh?

Mari Oh but Ray, it were crap awful weren't it, and you're on about putting us through it again.

Ray Mari, it's there, believe me. She's not a performer, I'll admit, no, but I can take care of that. Bear with me dove, while I work out the last details. I'm only gripping on to it so tight Mari, so pit bull tight, for all of us, cause I know it can take us to the top.

Mari Oooh. I love it when you talk swanky.

Ray If you knew how long I've been looking for summat like this. And here it is in me lap. (*Quickly.*) Along with you, along with you.

She giggles and buries her head in him. As she does he quickly writes more on the paper.

Ray Aye. Aye

Mari *comes back up.*

Mari You really is gone on this, ain't you Ray?

Ray I am dove, I've never had nowt decent to set meself on before, scrap, bent bookying, a bit o' this and that, clapped out old acts and knackered strippers.

Mari Don't. Don't do yoursen down Ray. You're Elvis in my eyes.

Ray Okay, granted, I might be the King of this gutter in which we live. But what's that? There's stuff above, love. Bungalows, gravel drives, Chateau Niff on tap, teeing off with Tarbuck and Brucie.

Mari Ooooh, hey. (*Sings.*) I did it my Ray. Oh there were times, I've had a few, bit off, bit off . . .

Ray Aye, aye, Mari. (*Shoving her off his lap.*) I've just got make a quick call.

She stands up.

Mari Okay, man o' mine, frigging go for it and you can depend on me. One hundred pesetas. In fact, I'll drink to that.

She goes off, still singing to herself, hunting for booze.

Ray (*through on phone*) Hello. Hello. 'Tape-deck', is that you? Yep, it's Ray. I'm calling in that favour you owe me . . .

Mari *is still singing and chucking stuff about at the back.*

Ray (*covers phone*) Mari, Mari. Here, look, here, (*Holding out a fiver.*) go down the offy.

Mari Ray, you're speaking my very language again. Tar.

She takes it, tries kissing him, phone wire getting caught up, etc.

Ray (*pulling away*) Aye.

Mari See you later, Ray-ver.

Ray Aye. Aye.

Mari (*leaving, stops at open door for an exit line. Overcome*) Sometimes, suddenly, life's nowt but holy in' it?

She goes. Pause. **Ray** *remains, looking at closed door in disbelief. Then turns back out front.*

Ray (*to himself*) Bloody hell. (*Back on phone.*) Meet me tomorrow down the club, okay. Bring your stuff. Just be there.

Puts phone down. Carries on scribbling.

Billy *appears in alley again, with a lamp, and shines light up into* **LV**'*s room, turning it on and off.* **LV** *comes to window. Opens it to see what's outside.*

Billy Over here. It's me.

LV Eh?

Billy Billy. LV, I've just been down the club after hours, to weigh up the space an all that for the light show. I got a shock. I saw 'Little Voice' on a turn poster, singing impressionist. Is it you?

LV You have lights. I have voices.

Billy Voices?

LV I sing in these voices. I . . . I hardly know I do it. It's just for me. Comfort. I . . . I . . .

Billy Hey, say no more LV. That's enough for me. I understand. But why you doing it down there?

LV They made me.

Billy Who made you?

LV Him and her. They go on until you do.

Billy Can't you say 'owt to make them see?

LV No one never listens to anybody but themselves, too loud.

Billy I do.

LV Yes.

Billy Are they trying to make you do it again?

LV She didn't like it. I won't be doing it no more.

Billy Oh well, that's good in it?

She nods.

Billy You do what's right for you Little Voice.

She nods.

Billy And cheer up.

She smiles.

LV Talk about the lights.

Billy Well, space down there is big enough. And it got me going. Aye, me brain came on straight away, making lights. Having a do wi' the dark. (*As though he's in the space.*) I thought, here, fwun. (*He swings his torch out over the audience in a beam of light.*) There, (*Swings beam in another direction, across audience, making a sound like a bullet.*) pkooo. (*Another direction.*) Here, zhum. (*Stops.*) I saw all sorts. It'll take some time though to fix it all up. Bloke said I can make a start any night as long as it's after hours. I don't know though. Would you be coming down? You never said you see.

LV I . . . .

She hears footsteps on stairs.

Billy What's up?

LV Oo somebody's coming. I got go now, will you come again, Billy?

Billy Yeah soon, soon as I can.

She quickly pulls window down and sits on bed.

Ray *knocks on door. Goes in.*

Ray LV, I've worked out the new act. You'll love it. Everything tailored to your personality. All you have to do is step on from the side.

She looks away.

Ray What's the matter? Hey, don't let a little hiccup like tonight put you off. Could happen to anyone.

LV Don't want do another.

Ray Listen, could happen to the best of them that. (*Pointing at albums.*) If you could ask her or her or her they'd tell you the same. They've had them nights an' all. Haven't you, Judy? (*Answering in her voice.*) 'I sure have Mr Say.' (*Laughs.*) How about you, Marilyn? 'Yes Ray, boo be do.'

LV Don't.

Ray Seriously, it'll never happen again, not with this LV. (*Showing paper.*) It's foolproof. Believe me. Let's do it eh?

LV *shakes her head.*

Ray Won't you even look at it?

LV *shakes her head.*

Ray Well, if that's what you want. (*Folds paper in half.*)

LV 'Tis.

Ray Okay. But it's a shame to just leave it like that. How about just giving it a try, just once LV. (*Holds up a digit.*) One more time and if it don't work out we'll forget it forever. I'll leave you to your records and your room.

She shakes her head.
Ray *folds paper again.*

Ray Fair enough, I've got me other acts, I'll be alright. I'll survive, so will you, it's just that . . . (*Looks at folded paper.*) Well never mind. Never mind then. That's that.

He folds paper completely and puts it in his back pocket.

Ray Aye, you've got it nice in here ain't you? Clean and tidy. (*Sits on her bed.*) All your records round you. (*Looks.*) Your Dad must a spent years building up this collection.

LV He did.

Ray I were never one for collecting things myself, only debts, I had an Auntie who was though. You'll never guess what she collected, go on.

LV What?

Ray Bluebirds. Wild bluebirds. Flying all round her house. Marvellous with 'em she was. You know she even got one of 'em to talk once. Yeah. Timid little thing it was, no bigger than your thumb, too scared to even leave its cage. And the way she did it were so simple. All she did was keep it shaded and safe at all times, sing to it, while stroking it, very soft, every day. And after a while it gave her its heart. And later, when it had grown strong, she set it free, but before it left, it stopped on the window ledge, turned, and to her great surprise sang. (*Sings*.) 'There'll be bluebirds over, the white cliffs of Dover, tomorrow . . .' See there she goes.

They both watch, as though they see it fly away. **Ray** *taps* **LV***, and smiles.*

Ray Eh, true that.

Ray *gently reaches down and picks up an album from a nearby pile.*

Ray Beautifully taken care of these, the covers and all that. Are you carrying on keeping 'em the same?

LV He showed me.

Ray Yeah, wiping 'em before play 'an all that?

She nods.

Ray Good thing. Collector's items some of them I imagine. Which were his favourites?

LV Them four there. (*Points to a pile*.)

Ray Ahh. (*Goes in pocket for paper, gets it out*.) Oh no.

LV What?

Ray Well. I was thinking we could a made sure we'd got them in, but we're not doing it now. (*Puts paper back*.)

LV Oh.

Ray Bet he would a liked that though, your Dad, eh? Tribute to his life's love performed by his only daughter. That would a been something wun't it eh? Sounds like he deserved it too. He were a good un eh, your Dad?

LV *nods.*

Ray I bet. Shame. Cause let's face it, the man and his music don't get much respect do they (*indicating downstairs*), if you know what I mean.

LV Ray.

Ray (*expectant*) Yeah?

LV Nothing.

Ray (*thrown, then . . .*) Look, there she goes again, the bluebird, under the moon and over the stars.

LV I'll do it.

Ray (*casually*) Oh, okay.

LV Only once.

Ray (*still casual, containing himself, not looking at her. Begins to leave*) Right then. I'm pleased. I'll just nip downstairs for me ciggies, back in a sec.

He goes halfway downstairs, stops. Faces out. Then, like a bastard.

Ray (*to himself*) Yes! Yes! Yes!

Blackout.

Lights up. The evening of the performance. **Sadie** *is helping to dress* **LV** *in* **LV***'s room. Quietly, caringly.* **Sadie** *has a fancy blouse on from 1964 or thereabouts, with ruffled frontage. She zips up* **LV**, *who is in a long, to the ground, incredible, figure-hugging, glittering, showbusiness dress.*

Suddenly **Mari** *comes bursting out of her room, struggling to do herself up.*

Mari SADIE! SADIE, come here. Where are you when I need you, frig!

Mari *carries on down to bottom of stairs, still struggling.*
Sadie *comes out the room and down.*

Mari SADIE!

Sadie *arrives.*

Mari Oh thank God for that, I need fastening up. It's harder and harder to get into this stuff, I tell you.

Sadie *does it for her.*

Mari Oh tar, well done Sadie, tar, here have a sherry for your accomplishments. Set you up for tonight as well.

Sadie Okay.

Mari Pour me one while you're at it.

Sadie Okay.

Sadie *pours two.* **Mari** *preens and lacquers her hair.*

Mari Fair old frontage on the blouse there Sade, eh?

Sadie *nods. Sits and sips her sherry.*

Mari You looking forward to going down there tonight then, Sadie? Yes. You stick with me, I'll make sure no one laughs at you.

Mari *lacquers more.*

Mari Ray's worked it all out. He thinks he's taking us all to Tarbyland. I had me doubts about her doing it again but, well he's won me over. I can't say no to him. Oh what a tongue that guy has, half raspberry, half razor.

Lacquers more.

Mari And I don't know, maybe for once that fucker fate is smiling down on us. How do you feel, Sade?

Sadie *and* **Mari** Okay.

Sadie Dokey.

Mari See, see. (*She carries on preening.*) There's certainly some raspberry in the air from somewhere. Oh, sod the devil, I'll put some bit more cheeks on.

She leans into mirror, putting make-up on.

Ray *comes in silently without her noticing. Puts sssh sign up to* **Sadie**. *Creeps up behind* **Mari** *with a necklace open ready to put round her neck. Just at that moment,* **Mari** *suddenly sprays lacquer, it goes all in* **Ray**'s *eyes.*

Ray Bloody hell. Aarrgh!

Mari Sorry. Oh my God. I've blinded my God. Oh no!

Ray *shutting and scrunching up his eyes.*

Ray I'm alright. I'm alright. Here, I got you something.

Holds out necklace.

Mari Oh, Raymondo, oh, oh. Look here, Sadie. (*Holds it to her neck.*) Fasten it for me, sir.

Ray Er. (*Hands out, then, finding something to wipe his eyes.*) I'm not coming near you.

Mari I'll do it then. (*She does.*) Looky here. Little sparkle neck me. See Sade. A love token. That's it in it, Ray?

Ray *nods.*

Mari In some ways, wish I could lash it round me finger. Ha.

Holds up engagement finger.

Ray (*to* **Sadie**) Well now Sadie, you're looking beautiful tonight love. Are we gonna get a dance down there tonight then. Eh?

Sadie *laughing.*

Mari (*quickly in*) Sadie, go upstairs now, see if she's ready, the star.

Sadie *does.*

Ray Can't wait Mari, can you? I'm buzzing fit to bust. Are you?

Mari (*unsure*) Yeah.

Ray What's up wi' you?

Mari Oh X-Ray, you can see right through me, can't you? It's just, what the sod hell are we to expect tonight?

Ray Mari. Mari, dove. Don't you worry 'bout a thing. All you have to do is be your radiant self as always.

Mari Aaay, Dr Ray, you can make me better with just a look and a word

She goes to kiss him but as she does, **LV** *appears on stairs.* **Ray** *moves away from* **Mari**.

Ray Aye, yes, hey, here she comes!

Sadie *brings* **LV** *down.* **LV** *dressed for performance. She is blank faced and looking 'not there'.*

Mari Aye, here she is.

Ray Let me open that door. The door that leads to success.

Ray *gets door.* **Sadie** *slips a plastic mac on* **LV**'s *shoulders.*

Mari Hey, get Sadie, the minder. (*She does a karate chop.*)

They set to leave in a procession almost. **LV** *looking down,* **Sadie** *behind her,* **Ray** *and then* **Mari**.

Mari And looky here, LV. (*Prinks necklace.*) Prink, prink. (*As they leave.*) As we leave, star spangling down the club, the artiste, the minder, the manager and the Mum.

Door bangs behind them. Lights of the house flicker, flicker but remain on.

Blackout.

The club. **Mr Boo** *at the mike.*

Mr Boo Testing, testing. Mr Boo here. Don't say my name too loud you'll give me a fright. No, now then. Ladies and gentlemen, forgive me if I get serious for a moment, what do you mean I never got funny? No, we've a return act for tonight, 'Little Voice'. I think you'll agree that last time the voice was there but the rest was little. Now I know we're a tough club, a hard club, and proud of it. And acts fall like flies in here. But I put in a plea if I dare for this girl. I put in a request if I may, for a bit of order, a little support if you could people, for the girl with the greats queueing in her gullet, shy little, Little Voice, ladies and gentlemen. Little Voice Hoff from down our way.

Ray *brings on a blindfolded* **LV**. *Lights illuminate a big barred, gold, cut-out cage. He leads her behind it, turns her* *upstage, back to the audience, removes the blindfold. He steps away. Signals for the music to begin. Exits.*

Orchestration of 'Goldfinger' begins. The cage ascends up and away into the skies. **LV** *slowly turns around. Sings abbreviated versions of the following songs:*

Shirley Bassey – 'Goldfinger'. (One verse.)

Shirley Bassey – 'Big Spender'.

Marilyn Monroe – 'I Wanna Be Loved By You'.

Gracie Fields – 'Sing As We Go'.

Edith Piaf – 'No Regrets'.

Judy Garland – 'Get Happy'. (With a big finish.)

Music ends. **LV** *in arms up, Garland pose. Blackout.*

Lights up.

They all burst in. **Mari** *first, then* **Ray**, *then* **Boo**, **LV** *and* **Sadie**. *They have loads of booze with them.*

Ray What about that, then?

Starts opening drinks. **Sadie** *gets* **LV** *to the settee and sits her down.*

Mr Boo Marvellous. Oh my God. Tears down cheeks.

Mari *screaming out.*

Ray See 'em all standing up. (*Imitates applause.*)

Mari *screaming out.*

Ray Here we go. (*Popping a shaken beer can, spraying everywhere.*) Ale and everything all round.

They all get into the drinks, except **LV** *alone on settee, staring out.*

Mr Boo Well, Ray, I can safely say your booking's assured down there. And have you, have you ever thought of the Monaco Club?

Ray Well, yes. Bloody, yes. Hey, Mari, we might be doing the Monaco Club an' all.

Mari *screaming. She puts the Jackson 5 on. Starts jiving with* **Sadie**, *who just remains standing still, with one arm out, while* **Mari** *does it.* **Sadie** *looks ill.*

Ray (*to* **Mr Boo**) Oh yes, Monaco for a bit, Mr Boo, I'll not say no, at this stage who would? But you know as well as me that soon not even the Monaco is going to be big enough for this.

LV, *exhausted, hears this, starts shaking her head. No one can see.*

Ray Mr Boo . . .

Mr Boo Do call me Lou.

Ray Mr Boo . . .

Mr Boo Lou.

Ray Lou, let me tell you. This is the greatest act going, this. We'll be in London before Christmas, or the cruises or the telly. Take it, take it from me.

LV (*shaking her head*) Once . . .

Mr Boo I hear what you're saying there Ray. But I hope you'll not forget where you got your start.

LV Once was said.

Mr Boo What was that, LV? What's she on about? I can't hear her.

Ray *is popping another bottle.*

Ray Is Sadie alright?

Mr Boo *looks too.* **Sadie** *looks a bit ill, and vacant, staring out.* **Mari** *stops dancing on* **Sadie***'s arm, and looks at her. Then to* **Ray***.*

Mari Sadie, Sadie May! She's alright. She's alright, aren't you?

She slaps **Sadie** *on the back,* **Sadie** *hiccups at this.* **Mari** *goes towards bottle* **Ray** *is holding, they all turn away to pour.* **Sadie** *has a little dribbly sick down her blouse. But just remains standing where she is.*

Ray We on for the whole week then, Lou?

Mr Boo It's yours Ray.

LV *passes out.*

Mr Boo I've cancelled the Silverados and Gringo Hodges to have it free for you. I couldn't do nothing else, they were going mad in there.

Ray I know.

Mr Boo Wouldn't leave me alone.

Ray I know. I saw.

Mr Boo 'When?' 'When's she on again?' and all that.

Ray *(drinks)* Yes. Yesssss!

Mr Boo *(to* **Mari***)* You must be proud, Mrs Hoff.

Mari *screams.*

Ray By the way, Sadie's been sick.

Mari Oh, bloody hell. (*To* **Sadie**.) Sadie! Sink and wipe. Sink and wipe.

Sadie *moves off on her own in direction of sink.* **Mari** *pours herself another.*

Mr Boo Well, Ray. (*Lifting glass.*) To the rise of Little Voice.

Ray (*raising his glass.*) Up tut' sky. Up tut' bloody sky.

Mari *turns just in time to lift her glass to join the others.*

Ray Cheers!

Mr Boo Cheers!

Phone rings. **Mari** *picks phone up. Screams down it. Puts it back down. Turns to see* **LV** *has passed out on settee. Looks again.*

Mari What's this. RAY! RAY!

Ray *comes over.*

Mari Oh God, has the little bird bleated and died wi' all the shock!

Ray She's alright. Just the excitement, that's all.

Mr Boo Loosen her clothes around the throat.

Ray *starts to loosen* **LV**'s *clothes.*

Mari (*stopping him*) I'll do that.

She tries but is fumbling, too drunk. **Sadie** *comes through, lifts* **LV** *and starts to carry her slowly upstairs.*

Mari (*taken aback*) Oh, aye, tar, Sadie.

Sadie *goes slowly upstairs.* **Ray**, **Mari** *and* **Mr Boo** *watching in silence, not moving, for as long as it takes for* **Sadie** *to carry her to her room.*

Mr Boo 'Blessed are the meek for they shall inherit the earth.' When, eh, when?

Ray Eh?

Mari *turns the record player back up.*

The lights blow.

Blackout.

Some days later. Evening. Alley lit by lamp only. **Billy** *is crouching there with a lamp, shining it on and off through her window. No response.*

Billy LV.

Flashes light.

LV.

Flashes light.

You're there.

Flashes light.

I know you're there.

Flashes light.

Can't you see me light? I've come every night since we last spoke.

Flashes light.

I'm worried. I know they're making you do it again and again and again. Are you alright?

Flashes light. Flashes light, almost like a morse code. No response.

The lights LV, I've gone ahead and started setting up. Getting stuff down. So much is needed.

Flashes light.

LV. I feel you flickering, fading away. I don't know how, it's like when one of my lights is ready to go, I feel it, I just know.

Flashes light, really fast one after another. No response. Starts to flash slow, slow again.

I know if I can get you to the lights they'll lift you. I know they will because I'm doing it for you. I've not said that to you yet, but I'm doing them for you.

Flashes light.

LV.

Flashes light.

LV. LV.

I'll not leave you, I'll be back.

He gives up, turns light slowly down, as lights come slowly up on next scene.

Lights up on living room. Some days later (same evening as the last scene), the evening of a performance. **LV** *is in her room in bed. All around her unopened presents. Bouquets of flowers beginning to fade. Downstairs,* **Mari** *sits on settee, looking out, drinking.* **Sadie** *is slowly making sandwiches on the kitchen table. Silence, except for the soft sound of sandwiches being made.* **Mari** *drinks.*

Sadie *works.* **Sadie** *finishes, puts last sandwich on plate, and begins to set off upstairs with them. As she passes* **Mari**.

Mari Here, give us them Sadie. I'll take 'em up.

Mari *takes tray and goes upstairs. Goes in* **LV**'s *room.*

Mari LV, love.

LV *is under covers, won't come out.*

Mari Come on, you can't stay there all day and night. I've brought you something to eat, you've got to eat, you've not ate now for four days. What about I put some music on then, some of your music, see what you think, eh?

LV *gives no response.* **Mari** *lifts the sandwiches above her head like she's going to throw them down.*

Mari I ready to throw these butties all over you. I will, you know I will.

She stares down, no movement. She sadly puts them on table by her and leaves.

Downstairs the phone rings. **Sadie** *answers it tentatively, unused to it, she listens.*

Sadie Hello. Okay . . . Okay! . . . OKAY!!

Mari *has arrived from upstairs.*

Mari That'll be Auntie. Pass it here. Auntie Slit, it's me Mari . . . No, I am Mari. Bloody hell. What? Yes. Yes she's on stage now Auntie, can you believe it? No you can't . . . Well it's right, our shy little LV is in showbizliness. I know what you're thinking. How long can it go on, well this is her fourth spot at the club and it's going down a treat and a malteser. Really, really, really they love her. Oh, I think so. Yes, she's fine, FINE! But you know what she's like. Anyway, tar for concern Aunt. Must dash now, yes. Woof woof. See you.

Mari *puts phone down and turns to* **Sadie**.

Mari She won't touch 'em, Sadie. She's not touched anything else we've left either, cup of stone cold tea there. She's on soon. She'll have to bloody go. I wonder if we're pushing her too hard, you know. One show after another. She'll not die, Sadie, will she? Die off? She's only frail, you know, like her Father was before her. Have a to ring Doctor Sock? I don't know. I'll wait for Ray, he'll be here in a minute. I don't know what to do any more. Come and sit by me, Sadie.

Sadie *does*.

Mari Look at me. Am I a good mother, am I doing right? I mean, she's making money now, I mean it's setting her off on something. In the long run, she'll thank me for it, won't she? There's always suffering and struggle in't there, and then they make it in the end. I've cheered up now. Tar for t'advice, Sadie. Don't know what I'd do without you. (*Half to herself.*) You patient fat get.

The phone rings.

She picks it up. **Sadie** *heads for stairs.* **Mari** *covers mouthpiece.*

Mari Are you going up for a go?

Sadie *nods.* **Mari** *nods.* **Mari** *speaks into phone.*

Mari Hello. Oh is that the local rag? (*Goes posh.*) No, no, she's not available for interviews, best try tomorrow, thanking you.

Puts phone down.

Mari Now then.

Door opens. **Ray** *comes in. Looking more affluent. He is smoking a cigar.*

Mari Darling.

She throws her arms round him.

Ray Alright Mari, alright. Where is she?

Mari Ray?

Ray Yeah.

Mari Er, don't know how to . . .

Ray What?

Mari Can she not have this night off?

Ray Not tonight, no. I've got Bunny Morris coming to see her, this could be a proper break. This could even mean telly.

Mari Telly?

Ray Telly.

Mari *runs to mirror and pokes her hair about.* **Ray** *goes to kettle.*

Mari Telly?

Ray Telly.

Ray *plugs kettle in, it flashes.*

You wanna watch that! Bugger me.

He rinses out a cup, has a drink of water.

Mari Ray . . .

Ray Yeah.

Mari Er, don't know how to . . .

Ray What?

Mari Any money sorted yet? I've only had a five and your dead Mam's necklace.

Ray Mari, I keep saying, leave it with me, it's all being carefully proportioned. Me and Boo is in fact just finalising a new contract. I'll let you read it when it's done.

Mari Oh no, no, no need for that. Just lob the doubloons into me open handbag when they's ready.

Ray Right then. You picked up them dresses from the dry cleaners, din't you?

Mari Oh.

Ray Don't tell me what I think you're going to tell me, please don't.

Mari *opening and closing her mouth like a fish, not knowing what to do.*

Ray Don't.

Mari *continues fish.*

Ray You forgot, din't you?

Mari *nods.*

Ray Oh no!

Mari I've been so busied, Ray.

Ray Bloody hell.

He boots the pouffe.

Mari Hey, watch me furniture!

Ray She's on any minute.

Mari I know! I know! Oh so sorry darling.

Goes to embrace him.

Don't be crossy wid your rolling puss puss.

Ray Never mind all that, she'll have to wear one of her old ones.

Mari Yes. Yes she must.

Ray What's she got?

Mari What's she got? What's she got? I don't know.

Ray Ooh!

Mari SADIE! (*Suddenly remembers.*) Wait a minute, I think there's one in the dirty wash.

Ray Bloody hell!

Mari It's alright, I'll iron it.

She gets dress out. Tries putting the ironing board up and nearly kills herself. **Sadie** *has arrived by this time. She and* **Ray** *watch in amazement.*

Mari Save me, Sadie! Save me.

Sadie Okay.

Sadie *takes over the ironing.* **Mari** *goes to* **Ray**.

Mari Ray Milland, you still my friend, an't you? Eh? Eh?

Ray We can't have this, Mari. I'm going to have to get someone else to look after her.

Mari What you on about, I'm her Mother.

Ray Are you?

Mari Yes. And you're my man.

Ray Am I?

Mari Ray, Ray, what you saying?

He walks away. She turns, kicks something flying, then turns to **Sadie**.

Mari You're too quiet to be my friend, you. Fuck off.

Sadie *goes.* **Mari** *picks iron up and starts ironing. She is slipping all over the place.*

Mari I'm doing it now, Ray love. Yes I am. I'll flatten it just so, once I've got me legs right.

Ray Leave it, you're gonna get burnt in a minute.

Mari *carries on frantically ironing, trying.*

Ray LEAVE IT!

She stops. Pause. He goes and gets dress.

Ray It'll have to do.

He is about to walk away, she grabs his hand.

Mari (*pleading*) Ray.

Ray Leave it, Mari.

Mari You're always rushing away, Ray.

Ray There's a lot to do.

Mari Ray, kiss me.

She strains towards him.

Ray Oh, get off.

Mari Ray?

Ray (*getting away*) Stop clinging on me!

Mari (*coming close again*) Don't spoil it, Ray! We go together so well.

Ray Go together well! Go to . . . Don't kid yourself
woman, we go nowhere. For a start, you're past it, your
body's gone. When your clothes go, I can't keep track
of it, it's all over the place. Too many maulings, Mari.
And you're too loud and you stink of drink. That's
alright for where you belong, the alley wall, the back of
a car, flat on your back on a rug. But no way could you
come with me and her to better things. No way love.
Look at yourself, look, lumping out your crazy clothes,
just about keeping your balance. Christ do you think I
don't have birds I go to, do you not think it's like
putting my face in flowers after you. You've had it
Mari, you're nowt now but something for after the
boozer, a chaser, a takeaway, a bit of a laugh. All
you've ever had that I want sits up there. And all
you're doing is getting in the way, woman. You were in
the way the night I heard her, that night I heard her
singing, and you're still in the way now. For godsake
wise up and fuck off.

He grabs up the dress and rushes upstairs. **Mari** *is shattered,
arms out in front, like a drunk lost thing, broken. Reaching out,
she walks out the door almost in a trance.*

Mari Sadie. Sadie. Sadie.

Ray *has arrived upstairs.* **LV** *is still in the bed.*

Ray Here, get this on, we're late. Come on. Come on.
I've had enough of you lot tonight.

LV *doesn't respond.*

Ray Dress on.

She doesn't respond.

Ray Get this on.

He grabs her up. She's limp in his hand. He slaps her. At that, voices begin to rush out of her uncontrollably, some sung, some spoken.

Judy Garland (JG), Piaf (P), Marilyn Monroe (MM), Shirley Bassey (SB), Billie Holiday (BH), Cilla Black (CB), Gracie Fields (GF).

LV (BH) 'Stop haunting me now, just leave me alone.' (SB) 'This is my life.'

Ray Hey.

LV (JG) Toto, Toto.

Ray Stop it.

LV (SB) 'Let me live. Oh let me live.'

Ray Stop it, I'm warning you!

LV (MM) 'Look what you started, a conflagration baby, that's what.' (SB) 'But if you go I won't cry.'

Ray Stop this.

LV (BH) 'You go your way and I go mine, it's best that we do.'

Ray Save it for tonight.

LV (SB) 'I, I, who have nothing, I, I who have no one.' (MM) 'But my heart belongs to Daddy.'

Ray Damn you LV.

Ray *is backing off a bit now with the sheer force of it.*

LV (CB) 'Something tells me, something's gonna happen tonight.'

Ray Oh no.

LV (JG) 'If you let me, let me, let me.' (SB) 'With my hands pressed up against the window pane.'

Ray Not mad. Not now please.

LV (P) 'Da Da Da Da Da Da . . .'

Ray Don't crack now, LV. Noo!

LV (P) '. . . Da Da Da Da Da Da.' Encore milord.

Ray No.

LV (MM) I'm tired of getting the fuzzy end of the lollipop.

Ray Please LV!

LV (JG) You go away or I'll bite you myself.
(SB) 'This is me. This is me.'

Ray Is it too late? Come back!

LV (JG) 'I guess when you met me it was just one of those things.'

Ray Oh my god. Come wi' me.

Ray *beckons to her.*

LV (SB) 'Beckons you to enter his web of sin, but don't go in.' (P) 'For at last I happen to be strong.'

Ray *is knocked back onto his knees.*

Ray I pray you LV. We was on our way together.

LV (JG) 'Happy together, unhappy together.'
(MM) See what I mean, not very bright. (JG) 'I'm going to haunt you so, I'm going to taunt you so, I'm going to drive you to ruin.'

Spins around and knocks **Ray** *who falls downstairs. He holds his mouth.*

Ray Me teeth.

LV (GF) Never mind your teeth, leave 'em out.

Ray *is at bottom of stairs. He looks up, she is still going from voice to voice, oblivious.*

LV (JG) 'Zing, zing, zing.'

She goes back in her room.

LV (CB) 'Step inside love, and stay, Step inside love, step inside love.' (SB) 'Just an empty room, full of empty space, like the empty look I see on your face.' (GF) 'Sally, Sally, pride of our alley.'

Ray, *devastated, rushes out, slams the door. With the force of the slam, the iron falls off the ironing board. Socket explodes. Light cracks and a flame rips around the ceiling and wall sides. A fire begins.* **LV** *in her room, still going from one voice to another.*

(JG) Run Toto, run Toto. He got away. He got away. (P) Bravo, bravo.

The sound of fire below, smoke is rising and into the room. She is oblivious to it. Smoke almost covering her.

LV (JG) 'Cos when you're crying, don't you know that your make-up starts to run, and your eyes get red and scrappy.' (P) 'Both the good and the bad I have flung in the fire.' (MM) 'But baby I like it hot.' (JG) 'Glory, glory, hallelujah, glory, glory, hallelujah, his truth is marching on.' (JG) I'm frightened Auntie Em, I'm frightened. (JG) There's no place like home. There's no place like home. There's no place like home. There's no place like home . . . .

Suddenly the 'Cherry Picker' appears high in the alley and glides up to the window. **Billy** *is in it. He breaks the window with his hammer, opens it and gets her out. Still she is going from voice to voice as the machine takes them away and down the alley.*

Blackout.

The club is packed. **Mr Boo** *excited and worried. His toupee on tilt. Sweat pouring off him. Caught in mid-speech . . .*

Mr Boo Calm down. Calm down. Sorry she's late. She'll be here any minute. I assure you. Look, sit down at the back! I never thought we could get so many in. What a star turn eh! Calm down. She'll be here soon! (*To someone.*) Look stop that! (*To someone.*) Put that back woman!

Suddenly, the opening strains of the song 'It's Over', Roy Orbison, come on from the juke box.

Mr Boo Hey get that bloody juke box off! Who's put that on.

Ray *comes toward stage.* **Boo** *sees him.*

Mr Boo Ray Say's here.

Ray *comes straight on, grabs the mike without looking at* **Boo** *and walks to centre stage,* **Boo** *following him.*

Mr Boo Where is she Ray? Where is she?

Ray *pushes him away.*

Mr Boo Hey, who you shoving. (*Sees something's up.*) What you playing at, give me that.

Reaching for mike.

Mr Boo Here.

Ray *suddenly threatens him, very violently, with mike held low like a broken bottle.* **Boo** *backs off.* **Boo** *signals offstage to someone. Then goes off himself.* **Ray** *turns to audience, dishevelled, some blood on his mouth and nose, sings to some of the lyrics, talks over others.*

Ray (*sings out*) 'Golden days before they end.'

Looking out into audience, hand shielding light.

Ray Bunny Morris. Bunny TV Morris. Where are you? Wherever you are. The bastard drinks are on me.

(*Sings.*) 'Your baby won't be near you any more.' Not tonight, not any night! (*Sings out.*) 'Tender nights before they fly.' Aye mine has. (*Sings.*) 'falling stars that seem to cry.' Aye true that's what they do. Can't hack it.

Ladies and gentlemen, I had a dream. (*Flicks mike lead. Sings.*) 'It's over.'

When I think what might have been. (*Spits.*)
(*Sings.*) 'It breaks my heart in two.'
Finished.
(*Sings.*) 'We're through.'
All through, THROUGH.

(*Sings.*) 'It's over. It's over.'

Suddenly juke box is turned off, record cuts out, he carries on.

(*Sings.*) 'Over, Over, OVER!!'

Stops, puts mike back in stand. Leans head on it. Long long pause. Silence.

Slowly he lifts his head. Slowly he walks off. **Boo** *has reappeared, we watch* **Ray** *go.*

Blackness. The same night. Later.

The living room is burnt out, charred furniture and soot everywhere, things melted and scorched. **Mari** *and* **Sadie** *come* *in silhouetted in door. It's too dark for them to see.* **Mari** *tries light switch. Nothing.*

Sadie I'll get me torch.

She goes.

Mari *strikes a match and sees everything. She gasps. The match goes out. She's still very shaken and slaughtered.* **Sadie** *comes back with a torch. Turns it on.*

Mari Look at the bloody crap of it. Me last home and testament gone up in flames, burnt to buggery. Sadie, I'm gutted. I'm gutted tut' twat bone wi' all this. Look at me ornaments, look at me home. Sadie, Sadie try getting some sugar now, it'll be caramel burnt. I tell you. You might like it, but I wouldn't. I wouldn't.

The phone rings.

Mari I told you about this phone din't I? Din't I? I knew it had some science to it.

She picks up melted phone.

Mari Hello, hell here. (*Listens.*) You got wrong number.

She puts phone down.

Sadie Who were that?

Mari Some official bastard wanting to know if Mari Hoff was still alive. Now then. Oh, Sadie, when I need picking up off the ceiling and the floor, who's left, but you, hey Sade? Hey, who thinks about me, but you. You're a friend, all lard and love, an't you? Come here. (*Hugs her.*) Sadie, your armpits have that smell of cat food again, what have I told you? Wash there.

Sadie Okay.

Mari Okay, rub-a-dub. Bloody hell, at least I'll be able to find you in the dark. Oh, what am I to do, Sade. Let's look up, might not be as bad.

They go upstairs. **Mari** *goes in her bedroom. Screams a little. Comes out.*

Mari All gone. Hopeless. Barbecued bed. Doorless wardrobes full of cinders. Sadie, where did I go wrong? Tipped from one trouble into another all my life. It seems I have to have the flames to feel alive but they always burn. Always burn me. Sadie, what's to become of me now? No house, I lost me job for never going back, no family, no man, where's Mr Ray now? Feeding somewhere else no doubt. Sadie, look at me. My hair piled crinkly on my head like a shock. Affixiated with years of lacquer. My skin creasing and folding faster than I can fill it in. Booze eyes and lashes, my lashes, my fifty lashes. Oh sod it Sade. Sod the whole burnt and choking chunk of my life so far.

She opens the door to **LV**'*s room.*

Mari Well, look at this, would you believe it? Only singed.

Sees records.

Mari Look, look what's not burnt.

She goes over to them.

Mari Look, the seeds of my downfall, the bitter beanstalk beaning circle beginnings that broke Mother's back. They go now.

She lets them fall out of their covers through the open window. They tumble into the alley and smash.

Mari Oh yes, they go now.

She sits on the bed punching the faces on the LP covers.

Mari You and you and you. You tooked my husband, played his heart till it stopped. You took my daughter, my walls. Take that.

She throws them out too, all out of their covers so they smash below.

Mari There, there. Down you go into smithereen alley. Crescendo. Crescendo on that hard gutter floor. I'm coming too.

She climbs onto window sill. **Sadie** *grabs her back. Holds her waist. She flops forward like a rag doll in* **Sadie***'s arms. Suddenly they hear a van pulling up. They look out the window.*

Mari (*to* **Sadie**) Out with the light. Hide.

They are heard scuttling about in the dark. Then stillness as the door opens and **Billy** *and* **LV** *come in. They stand silhouetted in the doorway.*

Billy I don't think you should be here. It's too dark. Come on away.

LV *just stands.*

Billy I'm not sure you should be.

LV *just stands.*

Billy Come on, let's go. You can get whatever you want tomorrow in the light. Come on, Little Voice.

Billy *turns to go, taking her with him. She stops him pleadingly.*

LV (*almost inaudible*) Please.

Billy I've some lights from work in the van, let me fetch them in.

He goes out. **LV** *stays in the dark.* **Billy** *comes in with the lights. When he puts them down, they illuminate the room, one* *orange, one yellow. They are the self-contained light units used around holes etc. They make the place look like a set for hell in an old theatre melodrama. Their faces are illuminated strangely from below in the orange and yellow lights and massive shadows are thrown up the back.*

Billy Shall I stay with you?

LV No.

Billy I'll wait outside.

LV No.

Billy You can't stay here on your . . . Okay, I'll nip back down the club. I'll finish off, then come back for you. Wait by the corner. Don't stay in here.

LV *doesn't answer. He looks at her. He kisses her gently on the face. He goes.*

LV *turns to stairs and makes her way up. Suddenly, bedroom door bursts open and* **Mari** *comes out.*

Mari What happened, eh? What happened here, then!

LV (*screams*) Aarrgh!

Mari The little match girl who goes burning everything, everything, everything down then.

LV *frantically shakes her head.*

Mari Yes. Yes. My house is a stub. My home a grate.

LV *steps back.* **Mari** *pursues her.*

Mari Now then girl.

Mari *almost grabs her. Suddenly* **Sadie** *sits up from floor.* **LV** *screams again.*

Mari Sadie!

Sadie Sorry.

Sadie *gets up and goes out.*

Mari (*to* **LV**) Where's your burns?

LV *looks scared.*

Mari Exactly. They is none.

LV *backs up.* **Mari** *charges at her.* **LV** *moves.* **Mari** *falls on settee. Mounds of soot fly up into the air, she can't be seen for a second, then the soot descends. She is sitting on the settee facing out. The orange and yellow lights strangely illuminating her face from below, her shadow thrown huge up the back.*

Mari I'm now in the carcass of my house, a smoked ham. I can't start again. What's the next move. I'm too beat for a man, really I ask you. I've been jumping the coals for years, now I've finally fallen in. Nobody wants the burnt bits, have you noticed. They love a blazing bint but when the flames have gone who wants the char? Well, some might say I've got what I deserve. But that's the problem, I've never had what I deserved. I was more than this dump I had to live in. In fact, my energy itself could have burnt this place down years ago, four times over with fireworks forever. I was more than what I married. Your Father, your Father kissing me with his parlour lips. I had health and breasts and legs. I strode. When I got behind your pram I propelled it about a hundred miles an hour. The air was full of the sound of wolf whistles, deafening. He was shambling somewhere behind, a beanpole Chaplin. But you, you were always his. It was always you and him, you and him all the time, doing quiet things, heads bent together, listening to the records. Driving me mad, my energy could have burnt this house down four times over, and you two tilted into books, listening the radio shows, playing board games in front of the fire. Fuck it. And now I'm dancing on my own grave and it's a roasting tin. My house gutted, my last possession gone. My last chance charred. Look at me up to my ankles in char. (*Looking at all the thick soot over the floor*). In fact, this is my soul leaking over the floor here, soot itself. I'm going to scoop handfuls up and spread it over you. Your head, you see, was the match head to this. (*Indicating everything.*)

She gets up with her hands full of soot, and traps **LV** *in a corner. Holding her with one hand while she prepares to cover her with the soot from the other, she holds her there, then . . .*

Mari Wait a minute. No. What do you want anyway? Oh, I know, your records.

She lets her go.

The firemen put all the salvage in the alley. They should be there.

LV *goes out and round to the alley.* **Mari** *stays put.* **LV** *sees the big pile of broken records almost filling the alley. Lamplight glinting off them. She gently picks a piece up. Opens her mouth to scream but nothing comes out. Opens her mouth again, nothing.* **Mari** *appears.*

Mari What's up, cat got your tongue?

Mari *steps forward but she slips on the massive pile of broken records, slithering all over in them and falls.* **LV** *quickly holds the sharp edge of a half record to her throat.* **Mari** *suddenly stunned.*

LV And now, you will listen! One time, one! (**LV** *screams.*) There's one. (*Screams again.*) There's another. Can you hear me now my Mother! (*Words rush out.*) My Dad, you mention him and it's wrong what you say, wrong what you say. You drove him as fast as you could to an early grave. With your men and your shouting and your pals and your nights, your nights, your nights, your nights, your nights of neglect. Things forgotten everywhere. No soap in the dish, no roll in the toilet, no clean blouse for school. Oh my Dad, when he had his records on he sparkled, not dazzling like you, but with fine lights, fine lights! He couldn't speak up to you, cause he must have wanted you so. I couldn't speak up to you, cause I could never get a word in! (*Looks at piece of record in her hand.*) These become my tongues. (*Drops it.*) And now they've gone, I don't know where this is coming from. But it's one after another and I can tell you now.

Pause.

That you hurt me.

Pause.

That you hurt me.

Pause.

With your sharp ways and the things you said and your SELFISHNESS WOMAN!

Pause.

I've got to stop now. I'm trembling so strange.

She drifts slowly away. **Mari** *on her knees, trying to stand. Pleading.*

Mari LV, I beseech you. I beseech you, LV.

Mari *is slipping, trying to stand but slipping in all the records. Soot all over her hands and face, in the lamplight, slipping, sliding, trying to stand.*

Mari I beseech you! I beseech you!

She stops struggling, flops face down in the pile.

Mari Slithered at last into the dirt gut of the twat of life, upended in an alley. I knew in my true heart there were nothing else for it, no matter how hard I tried I could not avoid what fate had reserved for me all along, the famous 'Tart's end', an old girl left dirty on her belly in an alley, homeless and juiceless and tootless and solid stone cold alone.

She closes her eyes. **Sadie** *is at alley end, peeping and softly giggling.*

Blackout.

Lights come up on the empty club. **LV** *comes in, stands at back of stage. Suddenly, faint purring sound of machinery.* **LV** *looks up.* **Billy** *comes into view in 'Cherry Picker'.*

Billy You come back on your own. I was just coming. Everything alright?

She nods.

I've just to fit this last un, then it's done.

He goes back up. We can't see him. **LV** *just standing, staring up at him, then all around, and at the stage where she suffered. He comes back down into view, this time continuing right to stage. Gets out.*

You sure you alright?

She nods.

You want to see display now?

She nods. He has installed his own expensive and amazing lights and effects into the club rig and all around. He operates them from a hand-held remote control.

Right. First a few lights.

He presses control, lights come on beautifully, spraying colours, then soaking the stage in deep blue.

And music.

He presses control. Powerful orchestral arrangement of Judy Garland song comes on. He changes lights again, again, through the building introduction, an incredible display. She is awestruck at it all, dizzied by it.

Sing if you feel like it.

She looks at him.

Sing Little Voice. Go on.

The lights suddenly become so powerful that they seem to lift her in the air, the music too. She closes her eyes, starts to sing, quiet at first, she opens her eyes to see millions of tiny white lights sprayed all over the stage. She sings louder holding up her hands like catching snow or stars.

Go on, louder.

He changes the lights again. She sings out.

Sing for yourself.

She sings out, stepping forward, louder, clearer as the lights beat and flash higher and higher weaving breathtaking patterns.

You're singing in your own voice. Your own.

She's singing full, confident, loud, tears coming down her face. She moves as she sings now. She's near the 'Cherry Picker'.

Get in. Go on. Go on.

She does. **Billy** *operates the 'Picker' it begins to ascend as she sings. Sings. The 'Picker' rising higher and higher. He changes to lasers, beautiful beams, breathtaking patterns across the space. She rises into them higher and higher, up in the lights, singing, singing, singing in her own voice.*

The End.

Production Notes

Music

All songs throughout the play should be suited to the
actress playing LV and the production:
The unaccompanied song, page 192.
The two performances, page 220 and 234.
The breakdown scene (sung and spoken), page 248.
The final song, page 261.

Although the choice of artists should remain in keeping
with the type of Diva and singer LV's father would
listen to, even a little opera may be appropriate.

Bearing the above in mind, any other music used in the
play can be a matter of choice.

The first act in the club (page 220) can have simple
accompaniment, (i.e. organ and drums) or be sung
unaccompanied, or a combination of these, i.e. the first
two songs accompanied and the last unaccompanied.

The second club act (page 234) should have an excellent
backing, live or recorded, or a combination of both.

The organ and drums, and drums alone, may be used
for music between scenes, if required.

Cuts and alterations to the text

In subsequent productions, the following cuts and
alterations were made to good effect.

Page 180, cut as follows:

Mari . . . or should I say Clark Gable.

She laughs.

Hurry up lads.

Page 182, cut Aunty Slit phone-call as follows:

. . . last glance upstairs, leaves. **Mari** *begins dialling.* **LV** *enters down the stairs. Picks up newspaper. Heads for kitchen.*

LV I hope you've paid for that.

Mari Oh shut up, it's me new toy and in fact . . .

Continues as written. If this cut is made, alter the following line on page 184:

Mari *sits on sofa.*

Mari Come on cock, make us a cuppa.

Page 185, cut as follows:

Mari . . . You emptied half the bloody bag yesterday. Do you like me phone?

Page 186, cut as follows:

Mari (*to* **LV**) Did you hear that. (*To* **Sadie**.) Bloody crazed chil' she is. She bugs me at times. Though I'm . . .

Mari . . . records her Dad left her, over and a over, on and on. That's not . . . . .

Page 186/7, the following, cut sequence, may be used.

Mari Go on, drink it now.

They both drink.

Mari Well, Sadie, what a night! What-a-night! What a championship neet! I copped off again with that Ray. I did it again! He had no choice Sadie. The club turn was a romantic singer, thank frig, and the music was in our heads, in our heads, and in his wandering hands. He knows so many people – 'Howdo Ray' 'Alright Ray'. You can see how I am there. Queen. Queen for the night. He motored me home about a million miles an hour, then screeching to a halt outside, did you not hear us? You must be dead if you didn't. I saw every other curtain in the bitching road twitch. Then he comes at me with this pronto snog, lip-lapping like hell.

That's men for you in it Sade, if you can remember.
Lip-a-lapping like old hell he was. But at least he's a lot
better than most, at least he knows how to slide and
dart and take a throat. At least there's always the thick
wad of his wallet up against your tit for comfort.

Sadie Aye.

Mari And he's got a finger in so many pies, Sadie.
Some too hot for his own good if you get my meaning.
In fact, he's moving into artist's management at the
moment, you know. Yes. He's got a crooner, a dog act
and two strippers at the moment. But he'll make it,
he'll make it in anything, Ray Say. See, that's why I got
the (*indicating phone*) ragbone in. I've got to be on call.
It's got to be smooth for him going out with me. I must
win him. I've got to keep him. He's got a lot of young
bitches into him a quart my age. I know they haven't
got my wizzle and mince but I'm taking no chances
Sade, how can I at my time of strife?

Page 190.

The film can be any film featuring one of the artists,
i.e. Gracie Fields.

Page 191.

The direction concerning the bottles may be shortened
to an action, where she goes to one place and gathers
up an armful of bottles, too many to hold properly, and
places them down on the coffee table. Backs off.

Mari There.

Page 193:

Mari's record should be someone like Tom Jones or
Barry Manilow or Julio Iglesias.

Page 193:
LV's singing must be orchestrated in with the dialogue
happening below so that Ray and Mari can be heard.
For example:

Mari . . . that's not the record, that's LV.
(**LV** *has faded her singing down to a low hum.*)

Scene continues to page 194:

Mari . . . could not succeed.

(*Song returns now, building up to volume.*)

Come on lover boy.

Ray (*still towards the singing*) Hang on, I'm listening.

Page 197:
The impersonation can be altered to anyone the actress
can do well. For example:

Ray . . . And of course Lulu.

LV Lulu?

Ray Yeah.

Continue as written until:

. . . *while he's distracted and not looking, she sings at full blast
the opening wail from 'Shout' by Lulu.* **Ray** *turns white.*

(Incidentally, the distraction direction given of the
wallet, can be anything that diverts him for a second –
cigarette, etc.).

Page 213: In some productions the whole of the last
scene of the first act (pages 213–18) has been cut
altogether, to very good effect. Act One then ends with
LV singing 'Somewhere over the Rainbow'.

Page 220: When the lights go out, it may be better to avoid total darkness so that the audience can just make LV out and see that she is singing.

Page 222: If the actor playing Billy is small, the following alternative may be used.

Mari Clear off. Go on. Shrimp on heat. Piss it. Go.

Page 230:
The effect of LV in the long glittering dress may be saved until later in the scene. If this is decided upon, then the scene should open with Mari rushing downstairs calling for Sadie. When Sadie appears, she comes running downstairs from bathroom or Mari's bedroom, as though she has been in there helping LV. LV then makes her first appearance in the scene when Sadie brings her down (page 233).

Pages 234/5:
The cage can be dispensed with, if preferred.

Page 241/2:
Cut the phone call, as follows:
She sadly puts them on the table by her and leaves. She goes back downstairs.

Mari She won't touch 'em, Sadie. She's not . . .

If the phone call has been cut, make the following addition to the speech on page 242:

. . . I wonder if we're not pushing her too hard, you know. Four, five spots at the club already. One show after another . . . .

Page 251:
If the production is using a revolve stage for the burnt out house, then the last scene in the club may be cut

altogether if preferred. What follows is another version
of the scene without juke box accompaniment.

The club is packed. **Mr Boo** *excited and worried. Sweat
pouring off him. Caught in mid-speech:*

Mr Boo She'll be here any minute I assure you all. I
never thought we could get so many in. What a star
turn eh! She'll be here soon. She will.

Loud scuffle and fight offstage.

(*Off mike.*) What the . . .

Looking off stage.

Ray! (*To audience.*) Ray Say's here.

(*Off, to musicians.*) Play the introduction. Play the
introduction.

LV*'s introduction music starts up.*

Here she is Ladies and Gentlemen. What you've all
been waiting for, the . . .

Ray *appears onstage.* **Boo** *still presenting, turns, is shocked to
see* **Ray** *on stage.* **Ray** *grabs mike without looking at* **Boo.** *He
is drunk, manic, blood round his mouth.*

Mr Boo (*angry, trying to get his mike back*) Hey!

Ray *bundles him in corner, head-butts him.* **Boo** *screams out in
pain. The intro music stops, discordant.*

Mr Boo (*holding his face*) Bastard. Bastard. (*Going off.*)
You're finished!

Ray *faces audience. Stares out.*
*Starts to sing, unaccompanied 'It's Over' by Roy Orbison. After
a few lines stops.*

Then, looking out into audience, hand shielding the light.

Ray Bunny Morris. Bunny T.V. Morris. Where are
you? Wherever you are, the bastard drinks are on me.

Continues with the song until he reaches:

Over, Over, OVER!!'

*Stops, lets his head drop on mike stand. Long, long pause.
Silence. Turns, walks slowly away.*

Page 260:

Cut Mari's last speech, so that stage directions run on:

*She stops struggling, flops face down in the pile. She closes her
eyes.* . . .

Page 260, final scene:

LV can approach the stage through the auditorium if
preferred.

Page 260:

If the Cherry Picker cannot be brought onto the stage
for the end, an ordinary, straight up and down lighting
lift can be used.

Methuen Modern Plays
include work by

Jean Anouilh
John Arden
Margaretta D'Arcy
Peter Barnes
Sebastian Barry
Brendan Behan
Edward Bond
Bertolt Brecht
Howard Brenton
Simon Burke
Jim Cartwright
Caryl Churchill
Noël Coward
Lucinda Coxon
Sarah Daniels
Nick Dear
Shelagh Delaney
David Edgar
David Eldridge
Dario Fo
Michael Frayn
John Godber
Paul Godfrey
David Greig
John Guare
Peter Handke
David Harrower
Jonathan Harvey
Iain Heggie
Declan Hughes
Terry Johnson
Sarah Kane
Charlotte Keatley
Barrie Keeffe
Howard Korder
Robert Lepage

Stephen Lowe
Doug Lucie
Martin McDonagh
John McGrath
Terrence McNally
David Mamet
Patrick Marber
Arthur Miller
Mtwa, Ngema & Simon
Tom Murphy
Phyllis Nagy
Peter Nichols
Joseph O'Connor
Joe Orton
Louise Page
Joe Penhall
Luigi Pirandello
Stephen Poliakoff
Franca Rame
Mark Ravenhill
Philip Ridley
Reginald Rose
David Rudkin
Willy Russell
Jean-Paul Sartre
Sam Shepard
Wole Soyinka
Shelagh Stephenson
C. P. Taylor
Theatre de Complicite
Theatre Workshop
Sue Townsend
Judy Upton
Timberlake Wertenbaker
Victoria Wood

Methuen Student Editions

John Arden	*Serjeant Musgrave's Dance*
Alan Ayckbourn	*Confusions*
Aphra Behn	*The Rover*
Edward Bond	*Lear*
Bertolt Brecht	*The Caucasian Chalk Circle*
	Life of Galileo
	Mother Courage and her Children
Anton Chekhov	*The Cherry Orchard*
Caryl Churchill	*Top Girls*
Shelagh Delaney	*A Taste of Honey*
John Galsworthy	*Strife*
Robert Holman	*Across Oka*
Henrik Ibsen	*A Doll's House*
Charlotte Keatley	*My Mother Said I Never Should*
Bernard Kops	*Dreams of Anne Frank*
Federico García Lorca	*Blood Wedding*
John Marston	*The Malcontent*
Willy Russell	*Blood Brothers*
Wole Soyinka	*Death and the King's Horseman*
August Strindberg	*The Father*
J. M. Synge	*The Playboy of the Western World*
Oscar Wilde	*The Importance of Being Earnest*
Tennessee Williams	*A Streetcar Named Desire*
Timberlake Wertenbaker	*Our Country's Good*

For a Complete Catalogue of Methuen Drama titles
write to:

Methuen Drama
215 Vauxhall Bridge Road
London SW1V 1EJ